Issues in Career, Technical and Vocational Education and Training

Lessons for the Caribbean

Edited by

Halden A. Morris

Order this book online at www.trafford.com
or email orders@trafford.com

Most Trafford titles are also available at major online book retailers.

Print information available on the last page.

ISBN: 978-1-4907-6582-2 (sc)
ISBN: 978-1-4907-6584-6 (hc)
ISBN: 978-1-4907-6583-9 (e)

Library of Congress Control Number: 2015917307

Trafford rev. 12/11/2015

 www.trafford.com

North America & international
toll-free: 1 888 232 4444 (USA & Canada)
fax: 812 355 4082

CONTENTS

LIST OF TABLES

LIST OF FIGURES

PREFACE

This edited book, *Issues in Career, Technical and Vocational Education and Training (CTVET): Lessons for the Caribbean,* emanated from a special assignment given to the first MPhil/PhD class in Education pursuing the leadership in Technical and Vocational Education and Training (TVET) and workforce development degree in the school of education at the Mona campus of the University of the West Indies, Jamaica.

The issues addressed in this book include teacher/instructor training, national qualifications framework, challenges for TVET to achieve the millennium development goals, quality assurance in TVET, revisiting apprenticeship from a global perspective, and challenges in the tourism industry in Jamaica. In this text the terms TVET, CTE and CTVET have been used interchangeably.

The first chapter, authored by the editor, focuses on preparing educators in CTVET for building human capacity, based on a Caribbean experience. Morris argues that it is only intelligent, highly skilled, imaginative, caring, and highly educated CTVET teachers that will be able to respond satisfactorily to the demands placed on education in developed societies. He identifies shortcomings of technical and vocational teacher training programmes that prepare technical personnel in the Caribbean.

The second chapter, authored by Wilbert Nunez, provides a historical reflection on the establishment of qualifications frameworks in CTVET globally. Nunes examines the global establishment of QFs from a historical perspective and explores the several challenges between input approaches and the recognition of qualifications and the learning outcomes. His research encompasses a desk review of case studies and research done by various TVET agencies and individuals with direct interest in TVET. Various case studies done on the conceptualizing of NQF and its relative importance in economic growth in Europe, Africa, Asia, the Pacific, Latin America, and the Caribbean are explored. He concludes by examining how NQF has impacted the various TVET systems globally.

Chapter 3, authored by Carole Powell, addresses challenges for CTVET to support the attainment of the Millennium Development Goals in the Caribbean. According to Powell, MDG number 3 specifically pledges to 'promote gender equality and empower women'. She argues that TVET has been promoted as a primary tool in the workforce development (WFD) strategy and is therefore a viable option to be employed in meeting the MDGs in the Caribbean. In respect of MDG number 3, after executing a comparative analysis which included Caribbean countries and two developed countries: New Zealand and the United Kingdom, Powell concluded that these developed countries with rich CTVET tapestry, definitely show the existence of more equipped women in wage employment, thus adding to the countries' economic success.

In chapter 4, Elaine Shakes explores the benefits of quality assurance in the management of twenty-first-century CTVET in Caribbean secondary schools. Shakes argues that secondary education is a fundamental conduit between the primary and tertiary stages in the educational hierarchy. It is responsible for the preparation of students for higher education and also the world of work. In reference to the renewed global prominence of TVET being recognised as the most profound strategy to accomplish and sustain the human capital in the twenty-first century, to achieve Education for All (EFA) and the United Nations Millennium Development Goals (MDGs), Shakes argues that a novel set of relationships among education, employment, and the labour market has been created. These new relationships, in addition to increasing globalisation, significant migration flows, international labour market opportunities, growth in international trade and services, and growing concerns regarding the quality of educational outputs, Shakes claims, are forcing institutions to adopt a system of agreed standards, quality, and recognition to empower them to adapt and respond appropriately to the socio-economic milieu.

Abdul Antoine investigates apprenticeship from a global perspective in chapter 5. He explores literature on apprenticeship training and various facets of apprenticeships. The articles predominantly focus on the merits of appropriateness to learning outcomes, workforce development, and benefits to persons, especially the youth. Some common threads that are evident throughout the literature are that the apprentice (a) is required to understudy a person who is both skilled and experienced at what he does, (b) understudies such a person for a prescribed period, (c) receives both practical and theoretical information, and (d) receives a stipend. In most cases, especially in developed countries, a legislative framework that underpins apprenticeship activities exists, which ensures constant monitoring and improvement, when necessary, in keeping with market trends.

Sheldon Thomas explores literature on the changes taking place in Jamaican tourism industry and whether the current state of the TVET system can prepare the workforce to deal with such changes in chapter 6. Research, he claims, has revealed that the current TVET system has been facing challenges, such as poor performance in numeracy and literacy, financing, lack of single qualifications framework, and poor matching of training programmes with labour market needs. He claims that partnerships with stakeholders will be important to address the deficiencies in the current TVET system to prepare a workforce that is able to meet the demands of the tourism industry.

It is anticipated that this book will be used as a text in tertiary level CTVET programmes internationally.

ACKNOWLEDGEMENT

Sincere thanks to the reviewers for taking time from their busy schedule to review chapters and provide timely and useful comments for authors to refine their work. Your timely contributions have been valuable and provided much guidance for the completion of the book.

Thanks to Mrs. Cecille Hemmings for conducting the peer review process and communicating with reviewers and authors.

Thanks to my wife Mrs. Carlene Morris for her timely suggestions and support as well as other family members, who exercised patience and provided encouragement while I produced this manuscript.

CHAPTER 1

Preparing Educators in CTVET for Building Human Capacity: A Caribbean Experience

Halden Morris

Human capacity development has been compromised in the Caribbean because of the lack of proper preparation of educators for Career, technical and vocational education and training (CTVET). Many have argued that the preparation of skilled workers is a key issue for the competitiveness of economies all over the world. The debates are focused on delivering quality teacher education for those who will be training future workers in the global economy while respecting the diversity of social, economic, and cultural situations.

CTVET teacher training programmes are also integral to producing competent academic professionals in most career, technical and vocational areas. The advancement of the teaching profession is of paramount importance to any nation. It requires intelligent, highly skilled, imaginative, caring, and highly educated CTVET teachers to respond satisfactorily to the demands placed on education in developed societies. This chapter will therefore identify the shortcomings of career, technical, and vocational teacher training programmes that prepare these professionals in the Caribbean, and make recommendations for improving these programmes to meet the demands of CTVET in the growing economies.

1.1. Introduction

In this chapter, the term technical and vocational education and training (TVET) includes career education. This is referred to as CTVET. TVET have been recognised as the primary avenue through which human capacity can be developed and is an essential element in the development of an economy. According to Morris (2012), the United Nations Educational, Scientific and Cultural Organization (UNESCO), the International Labour Organization (ILO), the World Bank (WB), and other multilateral organisations agree that over 80 per cent of all jobs in the world rely on, or are related to, TVET. UNESCO-UNEVOC (n.d.) has further emphasised that the qualification of skilled workers is a key issue for the competitiveness of economies all over the world, and the quality of teacher education is crucial in determining the skills of future workers. According to Schwab et al. (2002), TVET not only runs through a formal education system but also through an informal education and continuous training at the workplaces; this is also known as lifelong learning. Teacher or instructor training for TVET is, in some cases, offered 'in service', while in other instances, this is offered as a pre-service training. Irrespective of the modality of delivery, the value of this training is enormous as it relates to economic growth and development. The importance of TVET teacher training was emphasised by Zhao (2004), who stated that part of the important agenda of China is to increase interest in TVET teacher training in the country in order for TVET to act as a catalyst of national economic growth.

In the Lao People's Democratic Republic (Lao PDR), Soysouvanh et al. (2013) have noted that the strategic plan for the development of technical and vocational education and training, 2006–2020, lists the numerous weaknesses and the causes creating the low performance in the TVET system. As quoted from their Ministry of Education and Sports, one of the important reasons described by the plan for the weakness of the TVET system and the quality of teachers is as follows: 'The quality of TVET teachers remains mostly very low; teachers lack practical experiences, because they have not been employed in companies or enterprises and/or trained in the pedagogical field before' (MoE 2007, 8). They further claim that as a result of this, the Departments of Technical and Vocational Training (DTVE) and Higher Education (DHE) and the Ministry of Education and Sports (MoES) have articulated the goal, to be achieved by 2020, for vocational teachers as this:

> Building up vocational teachers for different subjects (technical and pedagogical) at different levels within the country and abroad in order to provide teachers for all TVET institutions sufficiently according to their demand; upgrading teachers for technical and pedagogical subjects and upgrading TVET managers and administrative personnel continuously in order to enable them to follow the ICT development. (MoE 2007, 11–12)

Soysouvanh et al. (2013) have emphasised that improvement of the quality and quantity of the education of vocational teachers is all-important. They have initiated studies to create standards for vocational teacher education at bachelor's level and to investigate the implementation and evaluation of measures for improving the delivery system.

The African Union (2007) has alluded to the trend of increasing awareness among policy makers in many African countries and the international donor community of the crucial role that TVET can play in national development. The increasing importance that African governments now attach to TVET is reflected in the increased emphasis on preparing teachers for TVET and the various Poverty Reduction Strategy Papers that governments have developed in collaboration with the World Bank and other bilateral funding organisations. The Jamaican government has also placed emphasis on TVET and, hence, teacher training for TVET. The minister of education, Hon. Rev. Ronald Thwaites, in addressing the nation on 20 March 2013 on CVM Television news about the placement of students in high schools as a result of performance in the Grade Six Achievement Test (GSAT) has pointed to the TVET division of the new secondary schools as an advantage since all students will be required to graduate with a skill from the secondary schools. This is a significant consideration since it places TVET as a priority for the education system in Jamaica.

Two critical and important features of TVET are their orientation towards the world of work and the emphasis of the curriculum on the acquisition of employable skills. TVET delivery systems are therefore well placed to train the skilled and entrepreneurial workforce that is needed to create wealth and assist in alleviating poverty. To this end, appropriately trained teachers will require the requisite knowledge and skills to be effective in the classroom. An important characteristic of TVET is that it can be delivered at different levels of competency and sophistication. This means that TVET institutions can respond to the different training needs of learners from different socio-economic and academic backgrounds and prepare them for gainful employment and sustainable livelihoods. It is therefore imperative that teachers are prepared to deliver training at all levels of the education system.

1.2. Pre-Service and In-Service Training of CTVET Teachers

As the terms imply, pre-service training is administered before the individual begins his teaching career, whereas in-service training is administered while the individual is actively involved in teaching.

Both modalities have been used successfully in several countries, such as Jamaica, Guyana, and other countries in the Caribbean.

Pre-service teacher training is provided to student teachers before they have undertaken any teaching. This modality is perhaps the most commonly employed in the training of instructors and teachers for TVET. TVET teachers and instructors who have completed pre-service training in the Caribbean are drawn primarily from high school graduates. These persons usually lack experience in the field in which they are being prepared. In some cases, they are allowed to enter the classroom to teach in their area of specialisation with absolutely no contact with the industry. The pre-service TVET teacher is usually given opportunities to develop their skills through lesson planning, teaching lessons and providing classroom activities, and in some cases, short attachment in the industry of their specialisation. The certificate received through this modality is usually recognised as the prerequisite passport to enter the profession of teaching.

The main objective of *in-service teacher training* is to develop the functional competencies of teachers that will enable them to actively and creatively participate in the further development of vocational education and training in their country. This approach requires a teacher training programme to embrace a dynamic approach that promotes a culture of continuous adjustments. To be successful, the programmes need to employ a systematic methodology in determining the needs and possibilities for professional development of the teacher. Instructors and trainers who access in-service training are at an advantage since they are involved in organised training while they are employed as a teacher/instructor in an institution. Additionally, these persons are usually highly skilled and knowledgeable from having completed an undergraduate programme that focuses on their area of specialisation before accessing pedagogy. In some developed countries such as Canada, Australia, and the United States,

CTVET trainee teachers are selected from the pool of technically trained personnel from industry and commerce who have made considerable contribution to industry/commerce. This approach ensures that all CTVET teachers are highly competent in their area of specialisations before they embark on their teaching career. Most in-service programmes are conducted with little to no connection with the pre-service CTVET teacher preparation programmes. The in-service training certification has been widely used as a quality control mechanism for CTVET teachers. It is anticipated that this training will improve the quality of the teaching process and, at the same time, provide an opportunity for persons to remain qualified as a teacher. In some instances, the in-service teacher training represents the first formal teacher training for instructors who enter the teaching profession with their technical degrees.

Preparing CTVET teachers and instructors presents challenges even in developed countries. This is because of the unique features of CTVET, which somewhat parallels the challenges experienced in the world of work. The actual task of career, technical, and vocational teaching embodies some unique features, such as (1) practical, hands-on activities; (2) highly regulated safety practices; (3) industry alignment; and (4) others, that clearly differentiate it from teaching in other areas.

1.3. Trends That Impact Teachers of CTVET

Delivery of CTVET teacher training internationally has been impacted by a number of trends. The trends include technology, workplace dynamics, professionalization of CTVET, changes in tertiary education, and globalisation among many other areas. Rapid development of new technologies requires that CTVET practitioners face new situations and interact in totally new environments, thus using skills that go beyond core teaching and learning competencies. The consequence of this is a more diversified role and work of the practitioners. Khambayat and Majumdar (2010) have pointed to Chappel and Johnson (2003), who have identified the typical role and work of the TVET practitioner. This, they claim, includes 'learning facilitator, workplace or industry trainer, workplace assessor, facilitator or consultant, and learning environment manager'. They claim that such diversified roles have required a new focus and thinking of TVET practitioners on their professional practice. They are now required to acquire skills that surpass the core teaching and learning competencies that they have obtained previously. Unfortunately, these targets cannot be currently achieved in Jamaica and the Caribbean because of the lack of opportunities for teachers to acquire skills outside the formal education system.

Internationally, the trend is towards further professionalizing the teaching workforce for CTVET. Many countries are making concerted efforts to increase the qualifications of their workforce and improve the continuing professional development (CPD) for their teachers and trainers. According to Weelahan and Moodie (n.d.), in Australia, the demands on TVET teachers and trainers are increasing as work changes, skill requirements increase, new industries emerge, society becomes more complex, and TVET is called upon to deliver more ambitious government objectives. This is reflected in the changing nature of TVET qualifications, which requires trained personnel/students to have the knowledge and skills necessary for the world of work. They also need the knowledge and skills required for further learning.

Weelahan and Moodie (n.d.) have claimed that the new Australian Qualifications Framework (AQF) will affect qualifications in all sectors since it requires the preparation of graduates for work or professional practice and for further learning. TVET must meet these diverse purposes and, at the same time, engage a wider range of students in learning, particularly those from disadvantaged backgrounds. It has been previously suggested that TVET has always engaged students from disadvantaged backgrounds, including trainees in the workplace who may also be disabled. Today there are increased demands on TVET to meet the needs of disadvantaged students and those in the community who are without foundation skills. TVET must also meet the needs of those who are already skilled to help them gain higher levels or different skills in order to support an innovative and flexible economy, as well as the needs of young people entering the workforce, older people who want to stay in the workforce, those already employed, and those who are not. These perspectives are congruent with those of TVET in Jamaica specifically and the Caribbean and developing countries in general.

CTVET must respond to the changes in tertiary education and, in particular, CTVET in higher education. These changes are driven by changes in the economy as well as by changes in government policies and the development of competitive markets. Occupational progression is increasingly related to educational progression, and the labour market destinations of TVET, CTE, and higher education graduates are less differentiated as diploma and degree graduates compete for the same positions. The foregoing suggests that CTVET must be configured to respond to a wide range of requirements and expectations. CTVET in schools is expected to play key roles in keeping young people engaged in education and in providing pathways to high-paying skilled work.

Yunos (2010), in his effort to define the requirements for TVET teacher training in Malaysia, has drawn attention to the Chilean and Korean experiences. He cites Rosedale's (2004) experience in Chile, where the TVET training system still lacks in preparation to fulfil the needs of the industry and individual satisfaction. Rosedale claims that the TVET teaching staff receives minimal formal practice especially in pedagogy aspects. As a consequence of this problem, the government has set up two TVET teacher training institutions in order to accomplish teacher training programme requirements. As Chae Ryang II (2004) has cited, South Korea's government, on the other hand, has provided a comprehensive training system that involves technical education and vocational training. Accordingly, South Korea has placed emphasis on the improvement of quality in the delivery of TVET teacher training.

Khambayat and Majumdar (2010) have identified five trends that they consider critical and will present significant implications for TVET teacher training (see table 1.1).

Table 1.1. Trends in TVET Delivery

Movement in Trends: TVET Delivery	
From	To
teaching-centred learning	facilitation-centred learning
teacher-centred learning	learner–centred learning
reproductive learning	productive learning
behaviourism	constructivism
time-based	outcomes-based

Programmes designed to prepare teachers for modern CTVET must take these shifts into consideration. The focus is no longer on the teacher, but instead on the student. The teacher is now required to facilitate learning by guiding the student in the learning process to be productive rather than just be reproductive. Other trends that significantly impact the delivery of training for teachers of CTVET include the utility of information and communication technologies (ICTs), the rapid expansion of the knowledge base in CTVET, and the increased engagement in quality-assurance activities.

1.4. New Developments That Influence CTVET Teacher Education

Although parallel to trends, new developments in information technology have facilitated new approaches in teaching and learning and are currently providing more widespread access to CTVET. The educational requirements for the workforce of the future are constantly changing, and information and communication technology (ICT) is being utilised as a tool to keep abreast of these changes. It is, however, evident that the use of ICTs in CTVET is very limited, since many issues are yet to be addressed. Some of these issues include the inability of CTVET teachers and trainers to apply technology in their teaching, the inability of teachers to access capacity-development programmes, the inability to localise and customise available resources to meet needs, the inability to develop content that enhances learning, and poor connectivity. It is evident that there is a need for the development and implementation of new educational practices to synchronise with new and creative developments in ICT and other technologies. As the commercialisation and globalisation of education expands, the pursuit of quality and the need to implement strategies for sustainable development have become urgent.

There is *rapid expansion of the knowledge base in CTVET* since many practitioners are contributing to the availability of information and data on CTVET through research and other data-gathering mechanisms. The introduction of new ICTs has had enormous impact on the availability of knowledge and information on CTVET. Additionally, the establishment of UNESCO-UNEVOC network and the development of advanced programmes in TVET in several universities all over the world have contributed significantly to the knowledge base. A most recent development is the establishment of a UNESCO-UNEVOC centre at the University of Technology, Jamaica, and the relaunch of the HEART Trust / NTA UNESCO-UNEVOC centre in Jamaica. It is anticipated that these centres will contribute significantly to the knowledge base in Jamaica and the Caribbean.

Increased engagement of quality assurance mechanisms for CTVET teacher preparation is evident in the Caribbean. This, perhaps, is fuelled by international requirements for the accreditation of CTVET teacher/instructor competencies. In most European countries, quality assurance of TVET teachers is a serious business. This process is regulated by ministerial authority. In most cases, for someone to become qualified as a TVET teacher, the authorities require both a university degree (or in some instances, a nationally recognised vocational qualification) and a specific qualification as a teacher. In addition, these teachers are usually required to have practical work experience since TVET teachers are expected to deliver training similar to that which is delivered by workplace trainers and instructors. While several national regulations impose varying requirements on staff involved in initial vocational training, there is no formal definition of the qualifications or formal training required for one to take part in continuing training.

1.5. Qualifications Required by Today's Teachers of CTVET

Today's international CTVET landscape requires that teachers and trainers are qualified as required by the industry and the education system of a country. In Jamaica, for example, the minimum qualification for a teacher is a bachelor's degree; consequently, it is required that teachers of technical and vocational subjects should have a minimum of a bachelor's degree in their area of specialisation. Additionally, there are several industry requirements/qualifications/certifications that should also be met. It is evident that there are several teachers in the system that possess the older qualification, which is a diploma in their area of specialisation; however, all new entrants in the system will require a bachelor's degree. Evidently, the qualification of teachers across the education system will be predicated on the level at which they teach. It is anticipated that teachers will be at least one level higher in the area that they are required to teach. The national qualifications framework (NQF) will provide further guidance on the qualifications of technical and vocational teachers for the various levels of the education system.

According to Management and Training Corporation (MTC), in 2011, many TVET instructors have not emerged from an academic background; rather, they have come from backgrounds where they have been content experts who have spent multiple years learning and refining their skills in a specific occupation. They typically have substantial knowledge of their craft but have never developed pedagogy or strategies of instruction. MTC has cited Frank Bunning and Zhiqun Zhao's (2006) work in which they have identified areas of competence in which all TVET instructors and trainers should be exposed. First, they should have an understanding of occupational profiles and content of the occupational field. Next, they should have an understanding of the analytic processes involved in shaping and organizing work processes, providing methodological competencies that are needed, and the changes that occur in the occupation, and finally, instructors must have an understanding of the object of professional work and must understand the processes and nature of the work and work environment, not just the subject area. Additionally, they should understand and be able to analyse, shape, and organise the occupation-related learning processes.

The training landscape requires a broader base for learners. There is greater demand for knowledge and skills needed for the workplace, and there is need for adequate language, literacy, numeracy, and foundation skills. Additionally, there is increased demand for technological and employability skills. As humans become more conscious of the environment, the need for 'green' skills increases, which has become increasingly essential for a sustainable economy and society. Training for CTVET teachers and instructors and, hence, their qualifications, has become increasingly complex. CTVET instructors must use their knowledge of the culture, economy, and context to develop learning environments that are appropriate for the occupational field. This is imperative since the landscape will differ in each situation. The competencies of the CTVET instructor must include the definition of educational goals, the selection of content and methods of teaching, and the ability to apply appropriate procedures for examination and assessment. These instructors should take advantage of programmes that prepare them for the information age and seek to utilise acquired knowledge and skills to improve the teaching-learning process of which they are an integral part. Qualifications in information and communications technology (ICT), robotics, simulation, and other cutting-edge technology should constitute a significant portion of the qualification of the TVET teacher (MTC 2011).

The Global Skills Network agrees with the foregoing and suggests that 'training providers need to have experience in the skills and knowledge they are teaching. And this needs to be hands-on experience in up-to-date industry practices and technologies. This can be a challenge even for trainers who have come out of the industry. They may have been teaching for some years and lost touch with the latest skills and practices. So a good relationship with industry can help trainers to keep their own skills and knowledge up-to-date. Often trainers will come through an industry pathway, from a "hands-on" background in the skills they want to train. Others might come from a teaching background. In this case they probably would not have had "hands-on" experience in the skills. Either way it is important for trainers to be able to develop and maintain their skills in a realistic work context so that they can effectively train others. This is the case even where there are occupational standards or competency standards in place' (p. 4). It is imperative that there are sufficient qualified trainers to meet the demand for training.

CTVET teacher qualification must embrace features that will satisfy the needs of the industries that the teachers will serve. Chief among these features are industry currency, pedagogical competency, and professional competence.

1.5.1. Industry Currency of CTVET Teachers

The importance of industry currency is critical for CTVET teachers, trainers, and educators. Maintaining industry currency is an ongoing process that requires the TVET professional to periodically engage himself or herself in appropriate industrial activities. A broader notion of industry engagement that goes beyond industry release include 'updating industry skills and familiarity with technological systems' understanding of big-picture developments in the industry; understanding of the entire industry sector, not just one section of it; understanding of developments in ways through which companies organise their businesses; global trends in the industry and the economy as a whole' (Smith et al. 2009, 89, in Wheelahan and Moodie, n.d.).

According to Wheelahan and Moodie (n.d.), Toze (2010, 8–9) has found, in a research conducted in Queensland, that trainers undertake a range of activities to maintain their industry currency, knowledge, and technical skill. They have concluded that activities should include industry placement or concurrent employment in industry and education, including work shadowing; membership in industry and professional associations; attending conferences, professional workshops, professional skills-development activities, and specialised training courses; carrying out research; and subscribing to professional journals and publications.

Trainers should constantly seek to upgrade themselves by applying for sponsored corporate teaching awards and scholarships. They should network with industry mentors, employers, and other trainers and talk to students about practices and job roles in one's workplaces. Toze (2010) further suggests that trainers should participate in industry specialist visits, industry site visits, and study tours and aim at fulfilling industry licensing or regulatory requirements. Opportunities such as research scholarships, international sabbaticals, cross-parish assignments, and involvement in industry projects can also be considered when planning industry currency activities.

Unfortunately, technical and vocational teachers, trainers, and educators in the Caribbean are not afforded the opportunity to establish or maintain industry currency. They are recruited upon graduation from the secondary high school system and placed in a 'pretrained teacher' training programme without any exposure to industry or commerce. As soon as they complete their training, they are employed to teach without any reference or linkage to the industry. Clearly, this approach leaves the teacher with little to no exposure to the real-life situation and places him or her at a disadvantage in the classroom or laboratory.

1.5.2. Pedagogical and Professional Competence of CTVET Teachers

It is evident that the global demand for qualified skilled workers has increased both significantly and rapidly. As this global demand for qualified skilled workers increases, so does the demand for competent teachers and trainers for technical and vocational education. This is particularly evident in developing countries, where governments are urged to accommodate the rapid development of TVET institutions both in terms of quantity and quality. This increase has moved significantly during the last two decades and has placed increased pressure on TVET teacher training institutions to increase the quality of their pre-service TVET teachers as well as their in-service teachers. This increase in demand has further prompted leaders of TVET systems to employ creative modalities for training teachers and instructors.

The professional and pedagogical competence of the technical teacher is crucial to the successful implementation of any TVET strategies. In this regard, governments should make conscious efforts not only to train new teachers but also to retain technical teachers in the system. To this end, Markovic and Axmann (2007) suggests that the initial strategy in teacher training should be directed towards achieving several objectives, including renewal and modernisation of the system of professional development and training, supporting the ongoing reform of vocational education and training, achieving a higher level of pedagogical skills and competencies of TVET teachers, introducing concepts of environmental protection and sustainable development into professional development and training programmes, and setting foundations for continuing education and lifelong learning.

Within Markovic and Axmann's (2007) strategy, the new concept of the development of vocational education, teacher, and instructor training can be accomplished using two modalities, namely, pre-service and in-service. In this regard, the 2012 Montego Bay declaration on TVET calls for the establishment of 'an effective framework for pre-service and in-service training for TVET Educators on TVET and Skills Development, embracing the competency-based education and training (CBET) approach'. If a framework of this nature is established, the Caribbean will witness a paradigm shift in the right direction where the preparation of CTVET teachers is concerned.

In discussing the professionalization of TVET teachers, Rauner and Dittrich (2006) put forwards four essential areas of responsibility for which TVET teachers should prepare themselves during their university studies. These include the following:

i. *The occupations and corresponding subjects of the occupational domain*

It is possible to assign twelve occupational domains to the twelve vocational disciplines. Characteristic for this first area of studies is learning about the occupations and subjects of an occupational domain as well as their genesis, the procedures of their development and evaluation, and the capacity to analyze local labour markets in order to draw conclusions for the training programmes to be offered by TVET institutions.

ii. *Analysis, design, and organisation of professional work processes*

This domain, which is central for the professional work of a teacher, comprises the ability to conduct labour and work process studies in the respective occupational domain and the knowledge of the contents and organisation of skilled work in the field. This area of study is of particular importance in the technical vocational disciplines since professional tasks undergo rapid changes due to the implementation of advanced technologies. As a complement to the analysis of changing professional tasks and qualification requirements, there is also the question of how to organise professional work processes—for example, implementation of lean management and effective structures of organisational development in the respective domain.

iii. The subject of professional work

Usually, we distinguish between service-oriented, economic, and technical occupational domains and vocational disciplines. TVET teachers must have sufficient command of the subject they teach with respect to the aspects of professional work in the domain under consideration. Whilst an electrical engineer, for instance, prepares in his studies for the construction of electrical processes and systems, a TVET teacher in electrical engineering has to study his discipline with a view to the selection, planning, configuration, installation, and maintenance and repair of electrical devices. In the same manner, the professional tasks of a medical doctor can be distinguished from those of a teacher who works in the education of nurses since the treatment of a patient by a doctor and the care for the same patient by nurses require quite different skills. This is why nursing has developed into an academic discipline of its own.

iv. Analysis, design, and evaluation of training processes

This area of responsibility refers to the didactic competence of TVET teachers. Studying this part of a vocational discipline qualifies one for teaching and for shaping learning environments in a given occupational domain. This includes the definition of learning objectives, the selection of teaching contents, using appropriate methods, as well as a command of the examination and assessment procedures.

It is essential that all CTVET teachers be equipped with these elements in their qualification to be effective in this era. It is also evident that a properly structured system will ensure that the youth, the poor, and the vulnerable of the society will benefit immensely from CTVET. The foregoing concurs with Morris's (1986) findings that teachers of CTVET in Jamaica should possess competencies in the following areas:

1. Programme planning, development, and execution
2. Instructional planning
3. Instructional execution
4. Instructional evaluation
5. Instructional management
6. Guidance
7. School-community relations
8. Student vocational-technical organisations
9. Professional role and development
10. Coordination

In addition to the foregoing, CTVET teachers should be competent in science, technology, engineering, and mathematics (STEM) in order to contribute significantly to the education of students in their area of specialisation. This is a critical requirement as there is heightened awareness of the importance of these elements in the training of smart CTVET personnel.

1.6. Standards for CTVET Teaching and Training

Yunos (2010) claims that the existence of standards is seen as a suitable solution to fulfil the specification and to implement a teacher training programme. He agrees with Moss et al. (1996) that standards is a basis of assessing characters needed to produce qualified graduates or with characteristics needed that meet the teacher training programme goal. He proposes a transnational standards framework for TVET teachers that focuses on six domains, including knowledge, skill, ethics and professionalism, social process, social accountability, and entrepreneurship. This framework can be used as a basis for establishing standards for

TVET teaching and training as the demand for personnel in this sector increases.

According to Knight and Elliot (2009), in the United States, research has begun to document the positive academic effects of vocational education graduates. Workshops have centred on integrating academics within vocational programmes, and a dual emphasis on graduates has emerged, one that touts entering the workforce and continuing education. The more the educational community has questioned the value of vocational education, the more it has become apparent that the new 'voc ed', now called career and technical education (CTE), has actually become more relevant today than ever. In the turbulent educational-reform world, other educational delivery systems have mirrored CTE, focusing on rigor, relevance, and relationships. The ultimate irony is that we have had the best and most effective teaching strategies since our beginnings, but because of what we have emphasised as determinants of excellence throughout our history, we have a ways to go to get others to believe that CTE has a place in today's educational settings for all students (p. 81).

In the Caribbean, the demands on CTVET are entering a new dimension. Governments are now beginning to understand the value of these types of education, and hence, they have heightened expectations from this training. With the establishment of regulatory agencies, such as the National Council on TVET (NCTVET), in several countries in the Caribbean, it is likely that quality will be assured. Additionally, the University Council of Jamaica (UCJ) and other accrediting bodies in the Caribbean are called upon to provide quality-assurance services for institutions involved in CTVET teacher preparation. The increasing diversity, however, makes ensuring quality and evaluating outcomes a major challenge, since trained quality-assurance practitioners in the field are few. This signals the need to provide additional training for CTVET teachers and trainers since they will be required to assume multiple roles and responsibilities in the quality-assurance arena. Multiple mechanisms should be put in place to ensure that they are equipped with the knowledge, attitudes, and skills required, which include a diverse range of teaching qualifications and continued professional development (CPD).

The CTVET educator for the Caribbean is faced with a radically different economy and society than others do in developed countries. They are faced with challenges that require a new set of skills that will have to be developed in as short a time as is possible. A primary focus is developing teachers and trainers that will prepare persons for the new workforce, as they are expected to train persons for employment in new jobs and for jobs that are not yet in existence. According to Khambayat and Majumdar (2010), key features include globalisation, ICT revolution, sustainable development, emergence of knowledge worker, and rapid knowledge obsolesces. New trends include climate change, disaster reduction, and emerging technologies. Khambayat and Majumdar (2010) identify elements of a TVET teacher's qualification standards, as depicted in figure 1.1.

In order to satisfy these standards, Khambayat and Majumdar (2010) propose two initiatives, which include capacity-building programmes for TVET teachers and the establishment of a worldwide TVET academy, that provide linking of regional organisations. Developing and implementing capacity-building programmes for TVET teachers will facilitate teachers in meeting standards established in the field. These programmes will take into account the weaknesses and gaps that exist and put in place mechanisms to address these deficiencies.

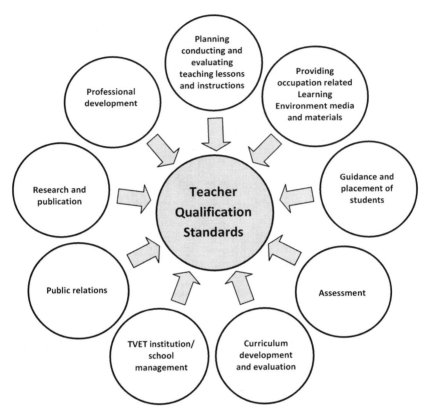

Figure 1.1. Elements of an emerging CTVET teacher's qualification standards (Adapted from Khambayat and Majumdar (2010))

It is evident that establishing a worldwide CTVET academy that links regional organisations will ensure international recognition of CTVET teachers and trainers. This initiative should be channelled through the Regional Coordinating Mechanism for TVET (RCMTVET), a body established by the Caribbean Community (CARICOM). An action such as this should be taken promptly to facilitate the preparation and recognition of TVET teachers and trainers in the Caribbean. Delivery of training for these teachers should be elevated to a position where it is not exclusively executed in underfacilitated classroom and laboratory/workshop settings.

1.7. Provision of CTVET Teachers and Trainers in Jamaica

It is evident that there is an enormous demand for CTVET teachers in Jamaica and the rest of the Caribbean. Several governments are coming to the realisation that this type of education cannot be ignored as a way forwards in building human capacity and equipping their citizens with the tools necessary for them to contribute significantly to the social and economic development of their countries. In an attempt to satisfy this demand in Jamaica, a technical teacher training programme was established at the College of Arts, Science, and Technology, now the University of Technology, Jamaica (UTech), in 1971, and the Vocational Training Development Institute (VTDI) was established to train vocational instructors. Soon thereafter, other Caribbean countries recognised this deficiency and requested UTech and VTDI to assist in preparing CTVET teachers and instructors for their territories. Having embraced a forty-year history of continuous provision of technical teachers and trainers for the Caribbean, the verdict is still out as to whether the objective of providing teachers to satisfy this demand has been met, since the output from these facilities has not significantly increased over the last thirty years while the demand continues to rise.

Details of the output of UTech for the years 2008 to 2012 is shown in table 1.2. The table further reveals that for the past five years, the institution has produced teachers in seven major specialisations, namely, business studies, computer with accounting, office systems technology, home and consumer studies, electrical technology, mechanical technology, and construction technology.

Noteworthy is the consistency in the average output of approximately 120 CTVET teachers annually, even though the output from each area of specialisation is rather inconsistent. Over the five-year period, only 37 mechanical technology teachers and 57 computer studies teachers graduated from the institution, whereas 200 business studies teachers and 118 family and consumer studies teachers graduated.

Table 1.2. UTech Pre-Service CTVET Teacher Output

Areas of Specialisation	Number Per Year					Totals
	2008	2009	2010	2011	2012	
Business Studies	56	42	43	24	35	200
Computer Studies with Accounting	18	6	19	8	6	57
Construction Technology	21	24	9	11	17	82
Electrical Technology	10	20	6	16	10	62
Home and Consumer Studies	20	29	18	23	28	118
Mechanical Technology	9	6	6	11	5	37
Office Systems Technology	19	18	9	9	14	69
Totals	153	145	110	102	115	625

These numbers correlate with the demand for CTVET teachers since just about all secondary schools have business education and home and family studies departments, whereas the other CTVET areas are not as common in secondary schools in Jamaica. However, the number of graduates has not grown over the years; in fact, there has been decrease in some areas. Additionally, there has been no addition of new programmes since 1990, even though the technical vocational landscape has changed significantly during the last two decades. It is evident that in order to build human capacity in CTVET for the Caribbean, there is a need to provide more opportunities for persons to be trained in this area. Technology is rapidly changing, yet the facilities for training CTVET teachers remained quite static.

1.8. Conclusion

Preparing educators for CTVET should not be taken for granted because of the pivotal role these persons play, as it relates to the economic development of a nation. These trainers and educators cannot perform their roles in social and economic development if they are not equipped with the knowledge, skills, and attitudes necessary for them to function effectively in their jobs. CTVET is considered a critical tool in eradicating poverty and in providing a base on which building blocks can be laid to stimulate the sustainable development of any nation. Unfortunately, in developing countries, this type of education is considered to be only for those who have failed in their academic pursuits. As such, only low-level skills are delivered through CTVET programmes, thus depriving the nation of access to higher-level job engagement and, subsequently, higher-level income.

There is need for expansion of teacher training opportunities in CTVET in the Caribbean. A most critical need is the expansion of training in emerging technical areas. The unavailability of teachers in these areas will have significant impact on the ability of the nations in the region to provide persons to produce goods and services that are required for sustainable national development. In Jamaica, for example, to support a logistics hub to accommodate smooth mobility of goods in the region, the need to provide technical personnel to support this development has become urgent.

If Jamaica and the Caribbean are serious about keeping abreast of the developing world in developing its human capacity and advancing their CTVET programmes, there is an urgent need to do the following:

1. Revise the curriculum for preparing CTVET teachers in new and emerging fields, including logistics, transport, robotics, ICT, management of hazardous materials, sustainable development, and other high-demand areas.

2. Provide opportunities and resources for trainers of CTVET teachers to study/upgrade themselves in the new and emerging areas.

3. Upgrade the existing training facilities by providing appropriate modern technology to deliver state-of-the-art training.

4. Expand the CTVET teacher training facilities to provide training for teachers in new and emerging areas.

5. Provide resources and scholarships for qualified students to access training programmes.

6. Forge relationships with industries and commercial entities to provide support in the provision of appropriate training for teachers and instructors.

7. Expand training in leadership in TVET, CTE, workforce development, and human capacity development to provide appropriate leaders in the workforce.

8. Create a coordinating mechanism or advisory body for CTVET teacher training.

9. Provide mechanism for appropriate quality assurance of CTVET programmes.

It is evident that immediate actions are necessary for Jamaica to make preparations for responding to the CTVET challenges that are on the horizon. If no actions are taken immediately, it is a certainty that the country will not benefit from the activities taking place around us.

1.9. References

African Union. 2007. 'Strategy to Revitalize Technical and Vocational Education and Training (TVET) in Africa'. http://info.worldbank.org/etools/docs/library/243614/TVET%20Strategy%20in%20Africa.pdf (viewed on 2 January 2013).

Coolahan, J. 2002. 'Teacher Education and the Teaching Career in an Era of Lifelong Learning'. Paris: OECD *Education Working Paper No. 2*. www.olis.oecd.org/OLIS/2002DOC.NSF/43bb6130e5e86e5fc12569fa005d004c/5b71d9d70e0f867cc1256c950053c48d/$FILE/JT00137131.pdf.

Global Skills Network. 2014. 'Five Critical Success Factors: How TVET Can Support Human Resources and Productivity'. Retrieved on 18 August 2014 from http://globalskillsnetwork.net/five-critical-success-factors-how-tvet-can-support-human-resources-and-productivity/#sthash.8H7BO8o1.dpuf.

Markovic, Jasminka, and Michael Axmann. 2007. VET Reform Programme—Phase II: Capacity Building and Implementation Support: 'Lessons Learnt in Vocational Education Teacher Training in VET Reform Programme—Phase II and Recommendations for Setting up a System of In-service Vocational Teacher Training'. Ministry of Education, Republic of Serbia. http://www.vetserbia.edu.rs/Zbirka%20dok%202/English/03/3/Lessons%20learnt.pdf (viewed on 2 January 2013).

Khanbayat, R. P., and S. Myumdar. 2010. 'Preparing Teachers of Today for the Learners of Tomorrow'. *Journal of Engineering, Science and Management Education,* vol. 2.

Knight, J. A., and J. F. Elliott. 2009. 'TVET Teacher Education: A Vision beyond Tradition'. *Journal of Technical Education and Training,* 1:73–83.

Morris, Halden A. 2012. 'Strategies for Enhancing Relationship of TVET Institutions with Industry'. Presentation at UWI/UNESCO Caribbean Conference on TVET, Hilton, Rose Hall, Montego Bay. 4–6 March 2012.

_____ 1986. 'Vocational-Technical Education Programme Components and Competencies Required by Teachers for Secondary and Technical High Schools in Jamaica'. PhD diss., Southern Illinois University, Carbondale, USA.

Wheelahan, Leesa, and Garvin Moodie. 2011. 'The Quality of Teaching in VET: Final Report and Recommendations'. Department of Education, Employment and Workplace Relations, Australian Government. http://austcolled.com.au/sites/default/files/quality_vetteaching_final_report1.pdf (viewed on 2 January 2013).

Management and Training Corporation. 2011. 'Training and Mentoring TVET Staff: Lessons from the Field'. http://www.mtctrains.com/public/uploads/1/2011/12/Training%20and%20Mentoring%20TVET%202011%20MTC%20Report.pdf (viewed on 2 January 2013).

Rauner, Felix, and Joachim Dittrich. 2006. 'Increasing the Profile and Professionalization of the Education of TVET Teachers and Trainers'. UNIP-United TVET Network on Innovation and Professional Development. In *TVET Teacher Education on the Threshold of Internationalisation*, edited by Frank Bünning and Zhi-Qun Zhao. UNESCO-UNEVOC.

Schwab, Klaus, M. Porter, and J. Sachs. 2002. 'The Global Competitiveness Report, 2001–2002'. Geneva: The World Economic Forum. 'UNESCO International Meeting on Innovation and Excellence in TVET Teacher/Trainer Education', in Hangzhou, China (2004). 8–10 November 2004 Hangzhou, China.

Soysouvanh, Boualinh, Bounseng Khammounty, Phouvieng Phoumvilay, Somlith Virivong, Ewe Elsholz, and Thomas Bohlmann. 2013. 'Developing Standards of Vocational Teacher at Bachelor Level in Lao PDR, Vocational Teacher Education and Research as a Task and Challenge for the East and Southeast Asian region'. TVET@Asia Issue 2. Retrieved on 28 July 2014 from: http://www.tvet-online.asia/issue2/soysouvanh_etal_tvet2.pdf.

University of the West Indies. 2012. 'UNESCO Conference on TVET and Human Capacity Development'. Montego Bay Declaration on TVET. http://www.soeconferences.com/tvet (viewed on 2 January 2013).

United Nations Educational, Scientific and Cultural Organization – UNEVOC (UNESCO-UNEVOC). n.d. 'Promoting Learning for the World of Work: Teacher Education and Training'. Retrieved on 18 August 2014 from http://www.unevoc.unesco.org/go.php?q =teachereducationandtraining.

Yunos, J. Md., E. Ahmad, R. Mohd, J. Mohd, and I. R. D'Oria. 2010. 'Transnational Standards Design Framework for TVET Teacher Training Programme'. IVETA 2010. http://iveta2010.cpsctech.org/downloads/materials/full%20papers/27.%20Transnational%20Standards%20Design-%20Md%20Yunos.pdf (viewed on 2 January 2013).

Zhao. 2004. 'Views from the Field'. UNESCO International Meeting on Innovation and Excellence in TVET Teacher/Trainer Education. November 2004, Hangzhou, China: 8–10.

CHAPTER 2

Establishment of Qualifications Framework in CTVET Globally: A Historical Reflection

Wilbert Nunes

There is a growing international consensus that mechanisms and systems for the recognition of qualifications need to be developed in cooperation in order to ensure fair and transparent decisions. There is also increased consensus that national developments in the field of qualifications frameworks (QFs) are both paralleled and supported by the emergence of regional frameworks. The understandings of regional qualifications frameworks as metaframeworks are also increasingly supported as a pragmatic mechanism to achieve regional objectives in the field of recognition of qualifications. This has led to at least six major world regions embarking on the development of regional qualifications frameworks that embody the promises of increased regional mobility and integration into international labour market schemes.

This chapter examines the global establishment of QFs from a historical perspective. It also explores the several challenges between input approaches and the recognition of qualifications and the learning outcomes. The research was carried out by completing a desk review of case studies and research done by various TVET agencies and individuals with direct interest in career, technical vocational education and training (CTVET). It examines various case studies done on the conceptualizing of NQF and its relative importance to economic growth in Europe, Africa, Asia, the Pacific, Latin America, and the Caribbean. It concludes by looking at how NQF has impacted the various TVET systems globally.

It is the expectation that this review will make a contribution to the existing body of available literature on QFs in TVET and will contribute especially to the reforms currently made by CARICOM countries. All discussions on TVET in this chapter applies to career education.

2.1. Introduction

According to the Organisation for Economic Co-operation and Development (OECD) (2007), a qualification is achieved when a competent body determines that an individual has learned knowledge, skills, and/or wider competencies to specified standards. OECD further contends that a standard of learning is confirmed by means of an assessment process or the successful completion of a course of study that results in the official recognition of value in the labour market and in further education and training. For individuals in the field of TVET, this becomes an important component of their qualification.

As postulated by Tuck (2007), a qualifications framework is an instrument for the development, classification, and recognition of skills, knowledge, and competencies along a continuum of agreed levels. These levels are usually agreed on by specialised bodies that determine the standards of competencies needed for the labour market. Within a local context, these standards are referred to as a national qualifications framework. The qualifications framework also indicates the comparability of different qualifications and how one can progress from one level to another within and across occupations or industrial sectors (Tuck 2007).

According to Shyamal et al (2009), there are three 3 pillars of the qualifications framework for TVET: (1) skills-based and work-related, (2) competence-based or outcome-based qualifications, and (3) quality assurance. They indicate that these pillars reflect the skills and knowledge needed to do a job effectively and show that a candidate is competent in the area of work that the National Vocational Qualifications (NVQs) framework represents. In general, this framework is based upon national occupational standards, which are statements of performance that describe what competent people in a particular occupation are expected to be able to do. They cover all the main aspects of an occupation, including current best practice, the ability to adapt to future requirements, and the knowledge and understanding that underpin competent performance. According to Shyamal et al (2009), the scope of frameworks may be comprehensive of all learning achievement and pathways or may be confined to a particular subsector of the education and training system—for example, initial education, adult education, and training—or an occupational area. Also, some frameworks may have more features or dimensions (e.g. credit or quality assurance criteria) and a tighter structure.

All qualifications frameworks, however, establish a basis for improving the quality, accessibility, linkages, and public or workforce recognition of qualifications within a country and internationally (OECD 2007). The framework should ensure that people can do more with their qualifications. However, it should be added that qualifications frameworks in practice are usually more than a grid of qualifications levels; instead, they typically have wider *political* and social aims and dimensions, such as seeking to integrate existing systems of education and training more closely. The policy priorities of most countries around the world presently include focusing on raising skills levels, reforming education and training systems, and improving qualifications systems. A particular concern for many countries is improving the relationships between education and training systems on the one hand and workforce on the other. Increasingly, qualifications frameworks are seen as useful policy tools to achieve these and other goals.

In recent years, there seems to be a dramatic increase in the number of countries adopting NQFs. The European Training Foundation (ETF), European Centre for the Development of Vocational Training (Cedefop), and United Nations Educational, Scientific and Cultural Organization's (UNESCO's) Institute for Lifelong Learning (UIL) (2013) indicate that 142 countries and territories are involved in the development and implementation of qualifications frameworks. These countries are to be found in all regions of the world and range from the most industrially and economically developed in Europe to fast-developing countries in Asia and developing countries in Africa and Latin America and the Caribbean. Increasingly, these national initiatives are being overtaken by cross-border or regional attempts to recognise qualifications.

The implementation of qualifications frameworks has also been widely endorsed by influential international organisations and bilateral agencies and is often supported by aid money and even loans (Allais 2010). This desk study was therefore undertaken to examine the establishment of a qualifications framework within a global context.

2.2. Historical Background of Qualifications Framework in TVET

The Context of Qualifications Frameworks

The origin of the qualifications framework is represented differently in related literatures. For example, ETF (2010) reports that the concept of qualifications can be traced back to the increased organisation of education in ancient civilisations.

According to Tuck (2007), the development of national qualifications frameworks (NQFs) has been a major international trend in reforming national education and training systems since the late 1990s. Across the world, many countries and regions are now not only talking about qualifications frameworks but are also either already implementing national, regional, and even transnational qualifications frameworks or, at the very least, are engaged in initial exploratory discussions, feasibility studies, and drafting of concept documents (Keevy and Samuels 2008). They have indicated that the initiative has first started and has been diffused mostly among English-speaking developed countries. However, since the late 1990s, such frameworks have also been adopted by non-English-speaking and developing countries.

Initially, the formal education system mainly dealt with philosophical, religious, ethical, and moral issues that eventually transformed into academic and practical skills. The term *qualification* started to establish proper meaning when universities were established in Italy, France, and England in the eleventh century (Higgs and Keevy 2009). Higgs and Keevy have further stated that the need for skilled workers has increased by the end of the nineteenth century, which has resulted in a move towards formal, structured, skill-related programmes through formal qualifications and, later on, emphasis on human capital theory and technological development. This theory has been identified as a key stimulus for economic development in the developing world, drawing predominantly from classical human capital theory, which is used to evaluate national skills development efforts. It determines the efficacy of these practices by matching workforce skills to the level of technological development and national training objectives. With an increased demand for transdisciplinary and multiskilled workers in the globalised environment by the end of the twentieth century, the formal education system has been viewed as limited and complicit in sustaining educational and social inequalities (Higgs and Keevy 2009). They argue that it is at this time the search for a more visionary or progressive approach to education and training has led to the idea of a national qualifications framework. Strong influences at the time include a call for the removal of the strong academic and vocational divisions between school and nonschool knowledge (Mukora 2007) and a move towards a competency-based vocational training model that advocated that 'qualifications could and should be expressed in terms of outcomes without prescribing learning pathway or programmes' (Young 2005).

Another example traces the origins of an outcomes-based approach to qualifications and curriculum to occupational psychology in the United States in the 1960s, where it was picked up in attempts to measure teacher competence based on political pressures, as education had come under public criticism (Young 2009; Spreen 2001). From there, the idea of specifying learning outcomes was introduced into vocational education (Jessup 1991) and emerged explicitly in the sixteen-plus Action Plan in 1984 in Scotland. This plan engaged all young people appropriately with an offer of learning or training between their sixteenth and twentieth birthdays and enabled support to be offered to young people more effectively beyond that age. This laid the basis for a series of reforms that led to the launch of the Scottish credit and qualifications framework in 2001 (Raffe 2003; Young 2003). Phillips (1998) indicated that the rest of the United Kingdom in 1987 was influenced by some of the ideas espoused in the 16+ Action Plans in the establishment of the National Council for Vocational Qualifications (NCVQ), which was created to develop 'a new system of qualifications that deliver the skills needed by industry'. This was implemented to influence the training for areas of employment within many industries. He further stated that initially, the NVQ framework was conceptualised to include all existing vocational qualifications, but instead, a new set of outcomes-based qualifications, alongside some existing ones replacing others, was developed. These two developments, the 16+ Action Plan in Scotland and the NVQ framework across the UK, as different as they were, are generally seen as the origins of the NQF phenomenon. This development influenced the establishment of frameworks in Australia, England, New Zealand, Scotland, and South Africa in the late 1990s (Phillips 1998).

In the late 1990s and early 2000s, frameworks started to be established in other countries. Much of this spread was in vocational education, often using the British NVQ model as basis. For example, when the first National Training Agency for Commonwealth Caribbean countries was established in Jamaica, it used a five-level framework based on NVQs. Barbados and Trinidad and Tobago followed suit. Both developments were based on competency-based qualifications developed through industry-driven processes (Holmes 2003). In some Latin American countries, frameworks of labour competencies were also developed, again influenced by the British NVQs, and competency-based training became a major feature of vocational education in Latin America (Vargas 2005).

In the late 1990s, what was referred to as the Bologna Process introduced the ideas of levels and outcomes to higher education reform in Europe. From about 2005, NQFs were developed in many countries in the Asia-Pacific region, particularly for vocational education.

2.3. The Establishment of Qualifications Framework in European Countries

There has recently been a dramatic increase in the number of European countries developing qualifications frameworks, following the adoption of the European Qualifications Framework

(EQF) by the European Union in 2008. According to Cedefop (2009b), all European Union countries are now signalling that they will develop comprehensive NQFs. Regional qualifications frameworks are also being designed or implemented in different places around the world, influenced by and influencing the development of NQFs. The European qualifications framework for lifelong learning has been adopted by the European Parliament and Council in 2008. It is aimed at post-secondary education and training and is described as a 'translation instrument'. This means that although it is called a qualifications framework, it will not be comprised of qualifications but will rather be the set of level descriptors that will be used to agree on common levels for qualifications across Europe. The framework has already been influential, leading to most European countries adopting an NQF. The EQF has also been used beyond Europe in the development of NQFs and is seen as the basis for regional frameworks internationally.

According to the ETF (2010), the European qualifications framework (EQF) was developed in response to requests from the member states, the social partners, and other stakeholders for a common reference to increase the transparency of qualifications. In 2002, the European ministers in charge of lifelong learning invited the European Commission, in cooperation with the member states, to develop a framework for the recognition of qualifications for both education and training, building on the achievements of the Bologna Process and promoting a similar action in vocational training.

In 2004, the ministers met in Maastricht, Netherlands, where they stressed the priority for developing an open and flexible European Qualifications Framework as a common reference for both education and training. In March 2005, following work undertaken by the European Commission, the EU heads of government formally requested the development of European

Qualifications Framework. The EQF was envisaged as a framework that would bring together three significant areas of policy development: the Bologna Process, the Copenhagen Process, and the Lisbon Strategy, initiated in 1999, 2000, and 2002 respectively. Presently, the EQF consists of thirty-one members, namely, Austria, Belgium, Bulgaria, Cyprus, Czech Republic, Denmark, Estonia, Finland, France, Germany, Greece, Hungary, Ireland, Italy, Latvia, Lithuania, Luxembourg, Malta, Netherlands, Poland, Portugal, Romania, Slovakia, Slovenia, Spain, Sweden, United Kingdom (EU member states), Iceland and Norway (European Economic Area members), and Croatia and Turkey (EU Candidate Countries).

2.4. The Establishment of Qualifications Framework in Caribbean and Latin American Countries

According to Morris (2013), the development of a national qualifications framework (NQF) from National Occupational Standards (NOS) is a key for linking training to certification. Collectively, NQFs will enable the development of a regional qualifications framework. The Caribbean Community (CARICOM) qualifications framework has been developed for vocational education in the Caribbean based on this approach. This framework is specifically focused on the adoption of competency-based education and training, which has been endorsed by the Council for Human and Social Development for vocational training in CARICOM member states since 2002. Adoption of this model includes accepting a five-level framework of occupational standards already developed in the region, accepting a process of standards development, and accepting a specific process of training delivery and assessment for certification (Zuniga 2003).

The support of the ILO Regional Office for Latin America and the Caribbean and IFP/SKILLS has enabled the ILO centre in the region to influence training based on competencies, quality of training, productivity, decent work, young people, gender, new information technologies, and e-learning, among others. In the framework of this cooperation, the ILO centre has been called upon to provide technical assistance in the planning, basic and logistic organisation of events, as well as coordinating their implementation and follow-up. According to an ILO (2009) report, there is an influence in the NQF across the region in Latin American countries like Argentina, Bolivia, Brazil, Costa Rica, and Mexico. The region has shown greater vitality, and as such, reforms have become consolidated, competency-based training strengthened, recognition of skills and competencies improved, and the approach of education and training systems are more strategic.

The countries that have started defining national vocational training (VT) frameworks have undertaken an arduous task, systematically adding further components to the discussion of the scope of training by competencies. Subjects like analysis of the national classification of occupations and its role as reference for competencies in countries, or the equivalences between academic careers and certificates in a consistent frame of reference, are currently being discussed. For instance, the INFOCAL foundation of Bolivia has adopted a system based on competency levels and areas of performance, incorporating a gender perspective; the SENAI of Brazil is working on a project for updating the Brazilian Occupations Classification with the Ministry of Labour; the SENA of Colombia has adopted a national classification and is endeavouring to extend it to statistical areas especially as a reference for its training offer in Chile, in the framework of the Chile Califica programme; and together with the Ministry of Labour and the Project Executing Unit, SENCE is studying different possibilities for updating the national classification of occupations and associating it with the national system of competencies. In the English-speaking Caribbean, the Human Employment and Resource Training Trust / National Training Agency (HEART Trust / NTA) of Jamaica has a national framework with five levels of qualification that is widely accepted and utilised by the CARICOM to promote manpower mobility and recognition of competencies. According to Zuniga (2003), there has been a documentation of these experiences, and they are made available to vocational training institutions (VTIs) that are increasingly interested in availing this instrument for modernising labour markets.

The Caribbean Community (CARICOM) was established in 1973 to, among other objectives, improve standards of living and work, expand trade and economic relations with third states, enhance levels of international competitiveness, and achieve greater measure of economic leverage (Tuck 2007). A regional meeting of heads of government in Grenada in 1989 resulted in the decision to deepen integration of the CARICOM region through the establishment of the CARICOM Single Market and Economy (CSME). The main focus of the CSME is to provide greater opportunities for employment, investment, production and trade, competitive products, improved services, opportunities for study and work between CARICOM countries, as well as increased employment. The main elements to introduce free movement of labour include elimination of work permits in a phased approach to designated categories of wage earners (e.g. non-graduate teachers, nurses, and artisans), mechanisms for equivalency and accreditation (mainly through the development of occupational standards and regional occupational certification and closer association between national training agencies), as well as the development of a skills register.

The CARICOM Single Market Economy (CSME) was created in 2008 (CARICOM 2008) and has since had a direct effect on the labour market and recognition of qualifications. An important factor to recognise in the CARICOM context is the homogenous nature of the region: all countries use English, most are island states (except for Belize, Guyana, and Suriname), and all face challenges of distance, dependent economies, and primary industries (Dunn-Smith 2009). Following agreement on a CARICOM Regional Strategy for TVET as early as 1990 (CANTA 2005) and the adoption of a competence model for TVET in 2002 by the CARICOM Council for Human and Social Development (COHSOD), the basis was laid for a CARICOM-wide TVET strategy based on the first NQFs in the region developed in Jamaica, Trinidad and Tobago, Barbados, and Belize. At this stage, the decision was made to structure vocational qualifications around five occupational levels. As noted by Dunn-Smith (2009), the threat of open borders and the need to improve the quality of the workforce required for education and training of all contributed to the demand for a regional TVET qualifications framework that would, in theory, be able to

- improve progression routes,

- modernise qualifications,

- ensure parity of esteem between vocational and academic routes, and

- promote transparency, comparability, transferability, and recognition of skills and qualifications.

The Caribbean Association of National Training Agencies (CANTA) was established in 2003 and endorsed by CARICOM as the implementation arm of the Regional Coordinating Mechanism for TVET (RCMTVET). The main agencies involved in the establishment of CANTA included the Human Employment and Resource Training (HEART) Trust of the National Training Agency of Jamaica, the TVET Council of Barbados, and the National Training Agency of Trinidad and Tobago. Currently, CANTA is composed of at least seven national training agencies and also includes TVET focal points in countries, as well as involvement from the Ministries of Education and Labour. The key purpose of CANTA was to establish and govern a regional training and certification system, called the Caribbean Vocational Qualifications (CVQs), to ensure standard and uniform delivery of competency-based training TVET within the CSME.

As part of this mandate, CANTA is to ensure acceptance and recognition of qualifications throughout the Caribbean and internationally. CANTA has also played an important role in the promotion and establishment of national training agencies through various capacity-building initiatives that have encouraged collaboration between member states, including the development of guidelines for occupational standards and for accreditation. In addition, CANTA has attempted to increase the number of member states that access CVQs, based on National Vocational Qualifications (NVQs) within member states. The fact that the Caribbean region has CANTA as a central coordinating agency is viewed by many stakeholders as a very important and positive feature of the CVQ framework. This is despite the fact that the funding of CANTA is a major challenge. At present, CANTA relies on subscription fees from member states, but this revenue is insufficient to establish a secretariat function. The development of CVQs has been preceded by regionally recognised school-leaving certificates developed by the Caribbean Examination Council (CXC). CXC has been largely successful in general subject areas but deemed inappropriate to the world of work, where the competency approach has been preferred (Gregory 2003), and hence lead to the development of CVQs (overseen by CANTA) from 2007 in a number of occupation areas: agriculture, business, communication, construction, energy, tourism, etc. CVQs can be obtained in schools on successful completion of all specified units. The CVQ certificate is awarded by the Caribbean Examination Council (CARICOM 2007), and the framework includes a common grid of skill levels for all qualifications:

- Level 1 (semi-skilled worker)

- Level 2 (skilled/independent worker)

- Level 3 (supervisor/technician/instructor)

- Level 4 (manager/entrepreneur)

- Level 5 (executive professional)

By 2010, a total of 672 CVQs were awarded in two member states: Trinidad and Tobago and Saint Kitts and Nevis (between 2008 and 2009, the majority of CVQs—97 per cent—were awarded in Trinidad). Of the 672 CVQs awarded, 275 were awarded in 2008 and 397 in 2009. The main fields wherein the CVQs were awarded were electrical installation, metal machining, and beauty therapy (Caribbean Examinations Council 2010).

According to CANTA (2005), the CVQ frameworks also allow for equivalencies to be established between elements of different qualifications and facilitate establishment of progression routes between different fields of study, such as general and vocational education, learning in initial and further education, and qualifications obtained through formal and non-formal education and training. Furthermore, CANTA suggests that the CVQ framework attempts to show the level of qualifications, pathways for improving qualifications, recognition, worth, and relevance of qualifications, and includes standards developed through consensus process among social partners and other stakeholders. According to CANTA, a key feature of the CVQ qualifications framework is the credible, fair, and transparent system of assessment of skills learned and competencies gained, irrespective of how and where learning has taken place.

The CVQ framework remains ideal for the region but with very limited conceptual work underpinning its development. With the exception of reports by ILO (2010) and the involvement of the majority of the CARICOM member states in the transnational qualifications framework (TQF) developed for the Virtual University for Small States of the Commonwealth (VUSSC)—which supports labour market mobility in these states both between and within countries and sectors by simplifying comparisons between qualifications and enabling a better match between supply and demand for knowledge—skills and competences, information on NQF development in the Caribbean, and the CVQ framework remain limited at best (Keevy, Chakroun and Deij. 2011).

Capacity within the CARICOM secretariat remains a challenge and, despite the noble efforts of a few dedicated staff, will require significant support in the future. The continued role of CANTA also seems to be at risk as funding remains a challenge and turnover of key staff. The radical transformation where education is 'measured in terms of standards, learning outcomes and competencies' is recognised within the Caribbean (Gregory 2003, 6). As existing expertise in the region, as well as the changed economic context, the challenges to CTVET for human capital formation, decent work, and employment, is recognised, a more holistic outcomes-based secondary education curriculum is advocated.

No specific resistance to the use of learning outcomes (which are linked to competency-based thinking) is reported, although it is emphasised that the region is still at a very early stage of development in this regard. The dominant historical paradigm in the Caribbean, as noted by Gregory (2003), was one of the comparative advantages. In this paradigm, it was recognised that none of the member states would be able to provide itself with the consumption requirements to ensure even the most basic standard of living, and hence, each member state was encouraged to engage in economic activities for which they were best suited (in terms of resources, labour, etc.).

Influenced by globalisation, the paradigm has made room for another, based on competitive advantage: in terms of human capital formation through education and training that nurtures and promotes individual and societal creativity, innovation, learning, entrepreneurship, and a quality workforce to create and exploit select global market niches (Gregory 2003, 4). This new paradigm has been realised through the CSME and continues to influence education and training in the region. International benchmarking is clearly being considered in the design of the CVQ framework, but this is limited to a technical exercise, as no intention has been expressed for a more substantial social strategy to build mutual trust, as is being followed in the European context.

Regional standards (such as the CXCs, CSECs, and more recently, CVQs) are seen as necessary mechanisms to improve the recognition of qualifications that are required to support the free movement of labour promoted through the establishment of the CSME. At the same time, it is noted that very few people have required CVQ certificates at this stage as these have not been widely implemented. Although intercountry migration is a key issue within CARICOM and has been addressed in part through the CVQ framework, international movement of individuals (in most cases, the highly skilled) is also a significant challenge. This factor may be partially responsible for the modest attempts at benchmarking the CVQ framework within the international context, as more substantial attempts, such as referencing of the CVQ framework to other frameworks internationally, may inadvertently contribute to increased outwards migration as a result of increased international recognition of Caribbean qualifications.

In 2007, the Council of Ministers of Education of CARICOM noted that the current five-level regional qualifications framework (RQF) of the Caribbean region was inadequate compared to that of other regions of the world, including African, Asian, European, and the Pacific states, which had been moving towards an eight- to ten-tier-level RQF. As a consequence, a working group was established to begin the process of updating the RQF to eight levels (CARICOM Qualifications Framework Workshop 2012). This has led to new developments, adopting the philosophical underpinning that the CARICOM qualifications framework (CQF) is to be informed by the principles of the 'ideal Caribbean citizen' who is expected to demonstrate that he/she is psychologically secure; values differences based on gender, ethnicity, religion, and other forms of diversity as sources of strength and richness; is environmentally astute; is responsible and accountable to family and community; has a strong work ethic; is ingenious and entrepreneurial; has a conversant respect for cultural heritage; exhibits multiple literacies, independence, and critical thinking in the application of science and technology to problem solving; and embraces differences and similarities between females and males. The CQF seeks to provide a broad framework within which these characteristics will inform the development of learning outcomes and assessment strategies at all levels of education and training systems throughout (CARICOM Qualifications Framework Workshop 2012). Although it has not been implemented officially yet, it is now in an advanced stage of development, and there is hope that with its implementation, this integrated framework will support the articulation between different levels and types of qualifications and the education system with multiple pathways to succeed in a context of continuous education in the region.

2.5. The Establishment of Qualifications Framework in African Countries

In Africa, there is generally a language barrier among the different countries due to the wide variation in linguistic traditions; however, qualifications frameworks developed in the Anglo-Saxon and French traditions are suitable for Africa. According to Keevy et al. (2011), the extent to which NQFs in Africa can be locally relevant, culturally appropriate, and based on African needs, perceptions, and conditions is foregrounded. Importantly, the contribution of NQFs to sustainability is viewed as closely interrelated with the need for Africa to learn and define its own qualifications values rather than to borrow policies from countries and regions that have already developed qualifications frameworks. Keevy et al. further states that it is in this regard that the position is taken that in order for NQFs to contribute to sustainable development, an unfettered diffusion from more advanced countries and regions will not suffice. It is posited that NQFs must become the expression of Africa's own preoccupations in order to contribute to sustainable development but that this position cannot be unconditional as it is influenced by several pragmatic considerations, not least being the global context that requires a common language to facilitate cross-border recognition and comparability of qualifications within, from, and to Africa. According to Keevy et al. (2011), in Africa, there are mainly transnational qualifications frameworks that are developed across borders. This includes regional qualifications frameworks where countries in the same geographic proximity collaborate to improve cross-border recognition of qualifications. The Southern African Development Community (SADC) and the Economic Community of West African States (ECOWAS) are examples of this type of framework.

In 1997, following the signing of the SADC Protocol on Education and Training, the SADC Technical Committee on Certification and Accreditation was established to oversee harmonisation and standardisation of education and training systems within the SADC region. The SADC Integrated Council of Ministers approved the development of a Southern African qualifications framework in June 2005. The focus was on technical and vocational education and training as well as in the promotion of the development of qualifications frameworks in individual countries. Its main focus was to ensure effective comparability of qualifications and credits across borders in the SADC region, to facilitate mutual recognition of qualifications among member States, to harmonise qualifications wherever possible, and to create acceptable regional standards where appropriate.

The need for harmonisation was driven by the huge diversity of education and training systems within member states directly as a result of the colonial legacy within the region; this ranges from Anglophone (such as Botswana and South Africa), Lusophone (such as Angola and Mozambique), and Francophone (such as the DRC and Mauritius) countries. A core objective of the technical committee was the development of a regional qualifications framework for the SADC region, the SADC RQF, envisaged as the most sustainable strategy through which the objective of the SADC Protocol on Education and Training could be achieved. At the time, the development of the SADC RQF remained largely isolated from similar developments in Europe and the Caribbean but was strongly influenced by the ongoing implementation of NQFs in South Africa, Namibia, and Mauritius. The extent of this influence has remained contested, more so as other transnational developments, some of which started much later, overtook the SADC RQF. A key factor in this regard was the decision to prioritise the development of NQFs in member states of SADC. The SADC RQF is presented as a home-grown strategy that has attempted to take the unique context of the region into account. In addition to the challenges of different levels of development and extreme economic disparities (for example, between South Africa and Zimbabwe), the different education systems (English, French, and Portuguese) within the region as a result of colonisation remains a key challenge.

Despite the various challenges, the effectiveness of the NQF has impacted South Africa mainly, with its implementation serving as an attempt to address the educational, social, and economic problems caused by apartheid. While qualifications frameworks seem to be driven by similar concerns in many countries around the world, the extreme inequality of the South African education system under apartheid as well as the extreme social and economic inequality in South Africa, the inefficiencies of the economy inherited from apartheid, and its rapid liberalisation after re-entry into the global economy, has made the NQF take on extraordinary significance in South Africa (Allais 2007b; Mukora 2007). The apartheid system in South Africa, described as 'the most notorious form of racial domination that the post-war world has known' (Thompson 1990), was officially established in 1948. The segregationist policies of the previous settler governments were consolidated with greater 'single-mindedness, consistency, and ruthlessness', as unwritten customs were enforced by legislation (Muller 1969). Laws were passed, governing almost every aspect of social life, ensuring that different racial groups remained separate, and confining black people to small parts of the country designated as black homelands. Officially, these 'homelands' were the national homes of all black people, including those residents of 'white South Africa' (ibid.; Denoon and Nyeko 1984). Education was used to reinforce lack of democracy as well as social and economic inequality by destroying and denying access to education, by providing poor-quality education to most black people, and by controlling the content of syllabuses to reflect the interests of the apartheid state.

The South African qualifications framework (SAQF) has been seen internationally as one of the most, if not the most, ambitious qualifications frameworks. Its main focus is replacing all existing qualifications in the country with a set of new qualifications designed by new structures; this was intended to ensure the overhaul of all learning programmes and curricula. At the same time, it was hoped to lead to new provision and new institutions as well as to many individuals getting qualifications based on knowledge and skills that they already had. Its designers and supporters hoped that by getting groups of stakeholders to create new qualifications and unit standards (part qualifications) consisting of learning outcomes, a qualifications framework could contribute to solving educational, social, and economic problems. Support for the NQF at its inception was described as 'extraordinary' (Manganyi 1996). Unfortunately, despite its noble and unquestionably worthy goals, its implementation had been fraught with problems. Shortly after implementation got underway, contestation and criticisms emerged (Allais 2003; Ensor 2003; Muller 2000; Breier 1998).

This has led to several commissioned reviews that have shown that there are 'broad malaise of discontent with SAQA and the NQF' (RSA Departments of Education and Labour 2003). Despite this discontent, the NQF has been implemented and is envisaged as a policy to underpin all other education and training policies; the NQF has been designed to use qualifications to transform South Africa's deeply fragmented and unequal education and training system, increase access, make education more democratic, but at the same time, ensure that education plays a role in improving the South African economy. Its stated objectives are to

- create an integrated national framework for learning achievements;

- facilitate access to education and training;

- facilitate mobility and progression within education, training, and career paths;

- enhance quality of education and training;

- accelerate the redress of past unfair discrimination in education, training, and employment opportunities; and

- contribute to the full personal development of each learner and the social and economic development of the nation at large.

In July 2004, a framework for qualifications in higher education was released by the Ministry of Education (RSA Ministry of Education 2004). This document, entitled the *New Academic Policy for Higher Education*, was enacted in a particular way for resolving the ongoing problems with the NQF. It indicated that the number of levels of the NQF would be changed from eight to ten. It contained draft-level descriptors for the higher education levels of the NQF.

2.6. The Establishment of Qualifications Frameworks in Asian and Pacific Countries

Under the Association of Southeast Asian Nations (ASEAN) Australia Development Cooperation Program, the enhancing skills-recognition systems in the ASEAN project was designed to assist ASEAN countries to keep their skills-recognition arrangements under review in order to meet emerging industry and employment needs across the region. A framework of occupational competencies at four levels of certification was developed at the semi-skilled worker, skilled worker, tradesperson/equivalent, and supervisor/equivalent levels. A regional qualifications framework was proposed.

The need for a qualifications framework is also considered for nations within the APEC (APEC 2009). The Pacific Islands countries are developing a unified register, Pacific Regional Qualifications Register, with the longer-term aim of expanding it to a qualifications framework. Parallel to this is the development of an inventory of technical vocational education and training programmes. The development of this register of qualifications by the South Pacific Board for Educational Assessment has been strongly supported by several Pacific Islands countries (Lythe 2008). A transnational framework is being developed for small (population-wise) commonwealth countries. It is defined as a 'translation instrument' and includes higher education and post-secondary technical and vocational qualifications. Many of these frameworks have been predated by conventions or declarations developed through UNESCO (for example, the Lisbon Convention and Bologna Process in Europe, the Arusha Declaration in Africa) that have aimed to ensure that countries recognised qualifications and part qualifications within different regions.

An APEC report (2009) indicates that the NQFs in operation in its member economies are diverse in their structure, coverage, operational purposes, and governance. The main aim is to provide greater transparency for qualifications, support for skills standards systems, and a means of managing quality assurance and to facilitate the international recognition of qualifications. The report indicates that economies use the NQFs as a basis for credit systems for transfer across education and training levels and institutions. Also, seven APEC economies—Australia, Hong Kong SAR China, Malaysia, New Zealand, Singapore, Thailand, and the Philippines—have NQFs. There are indications that the Republic of Korea is in the process of implementing one, and five others have them under development or consideration. Of the seven with frameworks, five have NQFs covering senior secondary, vocational education, and higher education qualifications, but there are differences in the framework across sectors. For example, in Singapore the framework applies only to vocational education and, in Thailand, to higher education. Five of the economies have explicit levels of qualifications, and two have them implicitly. Most NQFs contain descriptors of qualifications and units, and the descriptors are based on taxonomy of learning outcomes at least for the vocational education and training (VET) sector. Mainly, competency standards are the basis for qualifications and units in the VET sector. Most of the NQFs include measures of the volume of learning and a formula for estimating the amount of learning required to achieve a qualification:

- Credit frameworks have been developed in New Zealand and Singapore, and they are under development in some other economies.

- All the NQFs have an associated public register of qualifications.

- Recognition tools are being introduced in Australia and are under discussion in New Zealand.

- The NQFs in each economy are managed by a national agency.

- Compliance with the NQF is supported by systems of quality assurance, though its operation tends to be shared by a number of agencies.

- The frameworks have been supported by legislation or by government regulation.

- To date, the NQFs are not linked to regional or international frameworks.

It is the education and labour departments of the government that have been responsible for these qualifications. In several economies, NQFs have emerged from the CTVET sector associated with the developments of industry skills standards and competency standards–based qualifications. The introduction of competency-based training has been associated with a relative shift in control of the content of training from providers to industry. The autonomy of universities, who generally wish to retain the major influence on the content of their courses, has, in some cases, been a barrier to the development of an NQF, especially where the frameworks are accompanied by quality assurance and accreditation systems that are external to education providers. Quality assurance also takes several forms and improved registers of courses, and providers can be considered part of this.

Table 2.1 indicates the present status of NQFs worldwide in the form of first, second, and third generations.

Table 2.1. Generations of NQFs Worldwide

First Generation (implemented and started between late 1980s to mid-1990s)	Second Generation (implemented and started in late 1990s and early 2000s)	Third Generation (currently under consideration)
Australia, New Zealand, Scotland, South Africa, UK (excl. Scotland)	Ireland, Malaysia, Maldives, Mauritius, Mexico, Namibia, the Philippines, Singapore, Trinidad and Tobago, Wales	Albania, Angola, Barbados, Bosnia and Herzegovina, Botswana, Brazil, Chile, China, Colombia, Democratic Republic of Congo, Jamaica, Lesotho, Macedonia, Malawi, Mozambique, Romania, Serbia, Slovenia, Uzbekistan, Tanzania, Turkey, Uganda, Zambia, Zimbabwe

2.7. Reflection

Since the establishment of NQFs, it seems that their aim is to change education and training systems in a whole range of different ways globally in order to achieve desired effects, but it may be difficult to measure an NQFs impact on the performance of an education and training system since the concepts and categories used to measure performance may be changed by the NQF itself. What constitutes success can also be contested. It is also difficult to clearly argue whether or not a change in the right direction can be seen as due to the NQF or to other policy or institutional reforms. To add to these difficulties, the aims of some of the frameworks are very high level and ambitious, whereas the frameworks themselves are rather narrowly defined and technical. Nonetheless, strong claims continue to be made about what NQFs should be able to do. If policy makers in the countries that are now implementing or developing QFs are to learn from the experiences of earlier countries with qualifications frameworks, it is necessary to have some sense of whether they have in fact achieved their objectives and arrived at the interplay of factors that inform of their historical evolution.

There are indications that emerging NQFs reflect the national systems that they are supposed to operate within. While it has been observed that there are differences in specific objectives and in design features, it is generally accepted that frameworks need to introduce an explicit set of qualifications levels and level descriptors, that they must reflect the learning outcomes approach, and that a broad range of stakeholders from education, training, and employment must be involved.

The review also shows that countries have reached different stages of development and implementation and that more countries are now moving from early conceptualisation and design to stakeholder consultations and advanced testing of their frameworks.

2.8. Impact of NQFs

According to Allais (2010), it is too early to say whether or not the qualifications framework will achieve its goals. Nonetheless, some analysis of impact can be made in relation to the five earliest NQFs (the English NVQs and the Australian, New Zealand, Scottish, and South African qualifications frameworks). NQFs in Botswana and Mauritius have also been implemented for some time, and there are some lessons available. While the Malaysian NQF is new as a national comprehensive framework, it builds on previous frameworks and thus is drawn on to some extent. The labour competency frameworks in Chile and Mexico have also been under development for some time, and thus, analysis of impact and achievements can be made. South Africa seems to be the only country to have attempted a formal impact study. Various subsequent reports and research have suggested limitations with the impact study (Allais et al. 2009). A new study of the use and impact of the NQF has been initiated. Scotland has commissioned evaluations of its framework, and evaluations have been conducted in Mexico. There are few, if any, places in which successes and failures of the framework have been brought together in a clear and accessible format for practitioners and policy makers in the countries themselves, or in other countries, to learn from, even in the countries that have been implementing NQFs the longest.

2.9. Conclusion

The development of comprehensive frameworks requires clarification and, sometimes, redefinition of the borderlines between existing education and training subsystems. The relationship between CTVET and higher education (HE) indicates that the success of NQFs depends on their ability to involve stakeholders and to address conflicts of interest openly. The historical review of the establishment of NQF globally shows that the involvement of stakeholders varies significantly between countries. If a significant number of countries establish pro forma frameworks only loosely connected to the existing systems and practices, this can undermine the overall positive developments that currently can be observed. Overall, there is strong global momentum in developing NQFs. Whether this momentum can be sustained and strengthened depends on the involvement of stakeholders and the extent to which they see the added value of the NQFs. There needs to be a better understanding of the strengths and weaknesses of NQFs in order to actively support the rich and intense dialogue currently taking place globally in this field as well as inform national policy developments and reforms.

The support for the NQF remains strong, especially among employers and many providers. It is not yet clear what learners' experience is or what their views are, as many are still operating within old systems. Many new qualifications and associated developments such as partnerships are seen positively. There has been a beneficial impact on teaching, learning, and assessment practices. Integration of education and training remains problematic, and disparity of esteem continues to be seen as a barrier to portability and access to CTVET. Future revolutionary reforms must, of necessity, make reference to the historical establishment of QFs. This review will be useful in the context of Caribbean education and training reforms while advancing the body of existing information on QFs.

2.10. References

Allais, S. 2010. 'The Implementation and Impact of National Qualifications Frameworks: Report of a Study in 16 Countries/ International Labour Office, Skills and Employability Department'. Geneva: International Labour Organization (ILO).

———. 2007b. 'The Rise and Fall of the NQF: A Critical Analysis of the South African National Qualifications Framework'. PhD diss., School of Public and Development Management (Johannesburg, University of the Witwatersrand).

———. 2003. 'The National Qualifications Framework in South Africa: A Democratic Project Trapped in a Neo-Liberal Paradigm'. *Journal of Education and Work* 16, no.: 305–324.

Allais, Stephanie, David Raffe, and Michael Young. 2009. 'Researching NQFs: Some Conceptual Issues.' Employment Working Paper 44, International Labour Office, Employment Sector, Skills and Employability Department, Geneva.

Allais, S., D. Raffe, R. Strathdee, L. Wheelahan, and M. Young. 2009. 'Learning from the First Qualifications Frameworks'. Employment Working Paper no. 45. Geneva: ILO.

APEC Human Resources Development Working Group. 2009.

Breier, M. 1998. 'Three Questions for the Designers of the NQF'. in *Reconstruction, Development, and the National Qualifications Framework*, edited by K. Pampallis. Johannesburg: Centre for Education Policy Development and Education Policy Unit.

CANTA. 2005. CARICOM Process for Workforce, Training, Assessment and Certification.

————. 2012. CARICOM Qualifications Framework Workshop (11–13 July 2012).

Caribbean Community Secretariat. 2008. 'Single Market and Economy: Free Movement—Travel and Work'. Guyana: CARICOM.

Caribbean Community Secretariat. 2007. Launch of the Caribbean Vocational Qualification. Press release 258/2007, 23 October 2007. Remarks by Myrna Bernard.

Cedefop. 2009b. The Development of National Qualifications Frameworks in Europe. (September 2009). Luxembourg: Publications Office.

Denoon, D., and B. Nyeko. 1984. *Southern Africa since 1800.* London and New York: Longman.

Dunn-Smith, P. 2009. 'The CVQ: The Regional Qualifications of the Caribbean.' Presented at the Second Technical Meeting: Validation of the Guide for the Development of NQFs.

Ensor, P. 2003. 'The National Qualifications Framework and Higher Education in South Africa: Some Epistemological Issues'. *Journal of Education and Work* 16 (3): 325–346.

European Training Foundation (ETF). 2010. 'Inventory of Recent NQF Developments in the ETF's Partner Countries'. Working document for the EQF Advisory Group, 1 February 2010 (unpublished).

ETF, Cedefop, and UIL. 2013. Global national qualifications framework inventory prepared for ASEM education ministers conference: Kuala Lumpur, 13–14 May 2013 (asemme 4).

Gregory, R. 2003. 'The Role of TVET and the Caribbean Association of National Training Agencies (CANTA) and Allied Bodies within the Caribbean Single Market and Economy (CSME)'.

Higgs, P., and J. Keevy. 2009. 'Qualifications Frameworks in Africa: A Critical Reflection'. *South African Journal of Higher Education* 23 (4): 690–702.

Holmes, K. 2003. 'Qualifications Frameworks: Issues, Problems and Possibilities for Small States.'

Jessup, G. 1991. *Outcomes: NVQs and the Emerging Model of Education and Training*. London: Falmer Press.

Keevy, J., B. Chakroun and A. Deij. 2011. 'Transnational Qualifications Frameworks. Turin: European Training Foundation.

Keevy, J., and J. Samuels. 2008. 'A Critical Reflection on Current Qualifications Frameworks and Possible Future Directions in Africa'. *SAQA Bulletin* 12 (2).

Lythe, D. 2008. 'Qualifications Frameworks in Asia and the Pacific'. Geneva: ILO Regional Skills and Employability Programme for Asia and the Pacific, Supporting Skills Development in Asia and the Pacific.

Manganyi, N. C. 1996. 'The South African Qualifications Authority Act'. Paper presented at the Information Management Working Group on the NQF (IMWG) Conference.

Mukora, J. 2007. 'Response to Dr. Matseleng Allias'. Paper presented at the seminar held at the University of the Witwatersrand.

Muller, C. F. J., ed. 1969. *500 Years: A History of South Africa*. Third, revised, and illustrated edition. Pretoria: Academica.

Muller, J. 2000. 'Reclaiming Knowledge: Social Theory, Curriculum, and Education policy'. In *Knowledge, Identity and School Life Series*, edited by P. Wexler and I. Goodson. London and New York: RoutledgeFalmer.

Morris, Halden A. 2013. 'Revisiting Quality Assurance for TVET in the Caribbean'. *Caribbean Curriculum: UWI, School of Education, St. Augustine, Trinidad and Tobago 21*.

OECD. 2007. 'Qualifications Systems: Bridges to Lifelong Learning'. Paris: OECD.

Philips. 1998. 'Lessons from New Zealand's National Qualifications Framework'. *Developing Curriculum Standards: Lessons for Australia from Experiences in Other Countries*.

Raffe, D. 2003. 'Simplicity Itself: The Creation of the Scottish Credit and Qualifications Framework'. *Journal of Education and Work* 16 (3): 239–257.

———. 2009a. 'The Scottish Credit and Qualifications Framework (SCQF): A Case Study of a Very "Early Starter"'.

RSA Departments of Education and Labour. 2003. 'An Interdependent National Qualifications Framework System'.

RSA Ministry of Education. 2004. 'New Academic Policy for Higher Education'.

Shyamal, Rajesh, Tesoro, and Sorolla. 2009. International Conference on 'Harnessing Qualifications Framework towards Quality Assurance in TVET', December 1–2, Manila, Philippines.

Spreen, C. A. 2001. 'Globalization and Educational Policy Borrowing: Mapping Outcomes-Based Education in South Africa'. PhD diss., New York, Columbia University, Comparative and International Education.

Thompson, L. 1990. *A History of South Africa*. New Haven and London: Yale University Press.

Tuck, Ron. 2004. 'An Introductory Guide to National Qualifications Frameworks: Conceptual and Practical Issues for Policy Makers'. International Labour Office (ILO).

Tuck R. 2007. 'An Introductory Guide to National Qualifications Frameworks'. ILO.

Young, M. 2005. 'National Qualifications Frameworks: Their Feasibility for Effective Implementation in Developing Countries. Skills Working Paper No. 22, International Labour Organization, Geneva.

———. 2003a. 'National Qualifications Frameworks as a Global Phenomenon: A Comparative Perspective'. *Journal of Education and Work* 16 (3): 223–237.

———. 2009. 'National Vocational Qualifications in the United Kingdom: Their Origins and Legacy'.

Zuñiga, Fernando V. 2003. 'Lifelong Learning: Experiences towards the Development on NQFs in Latin America and the Caribbean'. CINTERFOR/ILO: Uruguay.www.cinterfor.org.uy.

Zuñiga, Fernando V. 2005. 'Key Competencies and Lifelong Learning'. Montevideo: CINTERFOR/ILO.

CHAPTER 3

Millennium Development Goal Number 3: Challenges for CTVET to Support Its Attainment in the Caribbean

Carole Powell

The Millennium Declaration by 189 nations was made in the year 2000 through the United Nations Development Programme (UNDP). The declaration was in the form of a pledge to free people from extreme poverty and multiple deprivations over the ensuing fifteen years. The pledge was translated into eight goals known as the Millennium Development Goals (MDGs), which would focus on three main areas of human development: developing human capital, improving infrastructure, and increasing social, economic, and political rights. All these are said to be in aid of the enhancement of the basic standard of living. MDG number 3 specifically pledges to 'promote gender equality and empower women'.

Career, technical and vocational education and training (CTVET) referred to as TVET in this chapter has been promoted as a primary tool in workforce development (WFD) strategy by several international development agencies. It has been promoted as a viable option to be employed in meeting the MDGs. This chapter investigates the viability of TVET as a tool for addressing MDG number 3 in the Caribbean.

3.1. Introduction

The Millennium Declaration by 189 nations was made in the year 2000 through the United Nations Development Programme (UNDP). The declaration was in the form of a pledge to free people from extreme poverty and multiple deprivations over the ensuing fifteen years. The pledge was translated into eight goals known as the Millennium Development Goals (MDGs), which would focus on three main areas of human development: developing human capital, improving infrastructure, and increasing social, economic, and political rights. All these had been said to be in aid of the enhancement of basic standard of living.

In the foreword of the 2010 MDGs report, the UN secretary general made the following statement: 'The Millennium Declaration in 2000 was a milestone in international cooperation, inspiring development efforts that have improved the lives of hundreds of millions of people around the world' (Ban Ki-Moon 2010, 3). Therefore, the progress seen should be sustained by increasing effort and drive to enhance human well-being. The eight MDGs are as follows:

i.   Eradicate extreme poverty and hunger

ii. Achieve universal primary education

iii. Promote gender equality and empower women

iv. Reduce child mortality

v.   Improve maternal health

vi.   Combat HIV/AIDS, malaria, and other diseases

vii. Ensure environmental sustainability

viii. Global partnership for development

When we look at the formulation of the goal statement, the verbs "promote" and "empower" imply 'to campaign for' and 'enable' respectively; these indicate processes that may be measured by a number of indicators. Hence, there is no foreseeable date of accomplishment, though there may be measureable milestones to indicate desirable behavioural changes and achievements resulting from the campaign.

TVET has been promoted as a primary tool in the WFD strategy for many developing nations and has been engaged in meeting the MDGs. According to Morris (2009), 'TVET is now widely accepted by developing countries as a critical tool in their efforts to eradicate poverty, enhance human development, and achieve Millennium Development Goals' (p. 1). This chapter investigates the viability of TVET as an important tool for achieving MDG number 3 in the Caribbean. The chapter will therefore define TVET and WFD, assessing their implications for MDG number 3 globally. It will then examine the current status of gender sensitivity, TVET, and WFD involvement in the Caribbean and at least two developed countries before making recommendations.

3.2. TVET, WFD and Their Implications for MDG Number 3

TVET, as viewed by UNESCO-UNEVOC (2011), ensures the acquisition of knowledge and skills to increase opportunities for productive work, sustainable livelihood, personal empowerment, and socio-economic development for men and women in both urban and rural communities. In UNESCO's revised recommendation (2001), TVET is understood as

1. an integral part of general education,

2. a means of preparing for occupational fields and for effective participation in the world of work,

3. an aspect of lifelong learning and preparation for responsible citizenship,

4. an instrument for promoting environmentally sound development (the greening of TVET), and

5. a method of facilitating poverty alleviation.

TVET is defined as this:

> A comprehensive term referring to those aspects of the educational process involving, in addition to general education, the study of technologies and related sciences, and the acquisition of practical skills, attitudes, understanding and knowledge relating to occupations in various sectors of economic and social life. (p. 28)

Developed countries like the United Kingdom (UK) and New Zealand have been said to owe much of their growth and stability to the prominence of TVET in their education system. The UK has been reported as having a robust education system, with TVET as a beacon in its curriculum. The British Council (2012) has stated thus:

> Vocational education and training is the key to developing the skilled and motivated workforce needed to maintain workplace standards, boost

commercial success and promote social cohesion. The UK is committed to skills development, and invests more than £60 billion on technical, vocational education and training each year. This has enabled the UK to develop an educational system that is internationally recognised for its high quality standards and its success in delivering the knowledge and skills that employers need to remain competitive and ensure a brighter economic future. (p ii)

With one of the most highly recognised education systems, New Zealand is reported to emphasise TVET in high schools as well as in colleges. According to a report on training by New Zealand College (2013), "the education ministry has taken up proactive measures to ensure that this form of education supports sustainable development in the nature-enriched country' (p. 1).

According to these defining views and telling statements on TVET in the two developed countries, it may be safe to conclude that this type of education, apart from being a power-driver for developed countries, if properly implemented, promises a solution for a wide cross section of socio-economic challenges that plague developing countries.

Giloth (2000) has expounded on the nature of WFD thus:

Today's workforce development implies more than employment training in the narrow sense. It means substantial employer engagement, deep community connections, career advancement, integrative human service, supports contextual and industry-driven education and training, reformed community colleges, and connective tissue of networks. (p. 340)

The National Centre for Education and Training on Addiction (2002) has described a WFD approach as moving the focus from individual factors for workers to also include organisational and structural factors relating to systems. It thus shifts the emphasis from skills deficit to systems enhancement. Some examples of individual factors are the knowledge, skills, and attitudes that TVET ensures. Examples of organisational and structural factors include policy, funding, recruitment and retention, accreditation, incentives, and resources in general. Thus, the scope for TVET has had to be significantly broadened since it is poised as a responsive tool for WFD. The formidable partnership between TVET and WFD is thus slated to address issues of social equity, foster substantial employer engagement, and promote alliances between competing social forces and educators. As a human resource strategy, WFD relies heavily on TVET as a discipline that sees to the acquisition of current and relevant knowledge, skills, and attitudes by individuals. The strategy incorporates a holistic approach that considers human barriers and how they affect the overall needs of a region. WFD thus informs TVET on content and its increasing responsibilities so that the discipline will in turn be better equipped to effectively play its role meticulously in the development of human capacity for the workforce. TVET and WFD therefore work in tandem to satisfy the main areas of human development, which, among others, encompass the ascertainment of equity in social, economic, and political rights as well as human empowerment. Hence, as a global HR strategy, the combine formed by TVET and WFD is expected to address the MDGs, specifically goal number 3.

MDG number 3 is concerned firstly with gender equality. The following statement offered by the World Bank (2012) in its overview of the World Development Report will clarify the true meaning of the term for better analysis in viewing its importance in contemporary global society:

Gender refers to the social, behavioral, and cultural attributes, expectations, and norms associated with being a woman or a man. Gender equality refers to how these aspects determine how women and men relate to each other and to the resulting differences in power between them. (p. 3)

Although gender gaps traditionally and globally weigh more heavily against women, the fact that the term *gender equality* takes into account the well-being of both males and females is very important to highlight in this current discussion since the traditional connotation unwittingly aligns the term to female-only concerns. The World Bank (2012) publication, in justifying the claim that gender equality is a necessity for development, has stated as one of its main messages that greater gender equality can achieve three major objectives for economic development:

1) To enhance productivity

2) To improve development outcomes for the next generation;

3) To make institutions more representative

Enhancing productivity. Women represent more than 50 percent of university students globally and 40 to 43 percent of the world's labour force. A significant volume of knowledge, skills, and experiences thus accrue to women because of their involvement in study and the labour force. It is perceived that productivity will be greatly enhanced if these acquisitions by women are to be fully maximised. This can only be achieved if women are allowed equitable access to inputs and facilities for production and services.

Improving development outcomes for the next generation. Improvement in women's health and education is perceived to be greatly linked to better outcomes for their children, according to studies done in Nepal, Brazil, Pakistan, and Senegal (World Bank 2012, 20). This is seen to be achieved by allowing women greater control over household resources, which has caused changing spending patterns in favour of children, thus enhancing the countries' prospects for growth.

Making institutions more representative. Substantial inclusion of women in economic, political, and social decisions serves to change policy directions and make institutions more representative of the population. A study done in India shows for example, that the inclusion of women's voices at the local level gives rise to increases in the provision of such public goods as water and sanitation because these commodities matter more to women.

The United Nations (2013) indicates that globally, the rate of female labour force participation has increased from 50.2 percent to 51.8 percent between 1980 and 2009. On the other hand, the male participation has fallen from 82 percent to 77.7 percent over the same period. The share of women employed outside of agriculture has risen to 40 percent although for southern and western Asia as well as northern Africa it has risen to only 20 percent The equity balancing in the workforce has come about largely due to (a) equity in educational preparedness of individuals, which is due largely to equity in access, and to the (b) relaxing of traditional cultural norms that reek of social inequities that are gender-based. In order to further address gender balancing at the workplace, the writers suggest that there is a need for transformational employer engagement, profound community connections, and integrative alliance of all players— i.e. employers, educators, and industry partners. The modern WFD thrust, backed by robust TVET involvement, now systematically employs access as opportunities by breaking down / eliminating some debilitating barriers, access as participation by supporting massive increases in training enrolment, and access as transition by fostering articulation within TVET tracks and into the workforce. All this effort encourages holistic policies that cater to all human groups at all rungs of the education/training ladder. However, as gender equity in access to TVET as opportunities and participation increases, due to traditional cultural norms in some countries, it is more difficult to create gender balance in the broadening of access as transition. This has led to lower rates in those countries identified in Asia and northern Africa.

The degree of successes gained in respect of goal number 3 throughout the 189 signatory states may be assessed by examining some of the country reports and updates that have been submitted and ratified. However, in United Nations Fact Sheet (2013), the UN has issued some general statements on where we stand globally. It has been indicated that the main avenue by which empowerment of women is to be achieved is through education and violence prevention and mitigation. With a target to eliminate gender disparity in primary and secondary education, preferably by 2005, and in all levels of education, no later than 2015, the UN has been able to offer the following facts, which have been summarised:

1. Steady progress has been made towards equal access of girls and boys to education, though disparities remain between regions and education levels, particularly for the most excluded and marginalised.

2. In primary education, gender parity has been achieved worldwide, and there has been great progress in attendance for both genders. However, in some African and Asian countries, girls continue to face barriers in this regard.

3. In secondary education, gains have been made towards closing the gender gap, which remains favourable for males, as girls still experience significant barriers, such as

domestic chores, child marriage, violence against girls, pregnancy, and disabilities.

4. At university level, access to education remains highly unequal.

In interpreting these facts, there is a level of promise, since there seems to be almost full compliance at the primary level at which much of the foundation work in educating begins. In time, it is expected that sequential education levels will be more adequately supplied with female population qualitatively and quantitatively. This should serve to encourage greater compliance in achieving the education targets.

Some UNICEF-supported programmes in various countries have been successful in mitigating barriers that maintain gender gaps in education. The following are some examples (UN Fact Sheet 2013, 2):

*   Scholarships for girls to fund registration, tuition, pocket money, bus fare, and uniform, including shoes, textbooks, supplies, and stationary. This has worked not only in enrolling and staying in school but also in effective class participation and progression to higher levels in education.

*   An online website that also works on a smartphone. It provides abuse hotline numbers and information about rights and responsibilities as well as support services for girls and women.

*   Training of women farmers in budgeting skills. With this training, women have been enabled to share in financial decisions and other such critical family decisions.

*   Training of women for representational politics and introduction of a quota system.

- Recruitment, training and incentivised employment of female teachers in areas of need.

In the empowerment of women, the UN Fact Sheet (2013) points to their status in the labour market:

a. Globally, the share of women employed outside of agriculture rose to 40 per cent, but rose to only 20 per cent in Southern Asia, Western Asia and Northern Africa. (p. 1)

b. Globally, women occupy 25 per cent of senior management positions. (p. 2)

c. The global share of women in parliament continues to rise slowly and reached 20 per cent in 2012. This is far short of gender parity, though an increase of one percentage point was seen during that year. (p. 1)

The global snapshot suggests that it is through education and training that gender equity and empowerment of women will be improved. Men and women ought to be empowered so that they will take their place in the society equitably and rightfully add value to the workforce. This has strong implications for TVET and WFD. The question is, as signatory to the MDG pledge, how well does progress within the Caribbean fit into the global picture as far as achieving goal number 3 is concerned, and to what extent can the increased involvement in TVET become a factor in achieving this goal?

3.3. Current Status on TVET Involvement within the Caribbean

The latter part of the twentieth century ushered in the regime of independent Caribbean nation states, which saw to an upgrading of the formalised TVET system, and the first technical school became a high school. The technical high school offered a complementary mix of academic courses, technological and practical programmes. A number of new technical high schools were later established as regional communications heightened. Hence, TVET in its modern form within the region resulted. According to Gregory (2003),

> Since the May 1990 launch of CARICOM Regional Strategy for TVET, the member states of the community have gradually being seized with the reality that the workforces of the region and by extension the economies of the region are at a competitive disadvantage, in relation to other workforces with whom the region trades and competes. (p. 1)

In view of this awareness, TVET development in terms of structure and form ensued throughout the region. The most formidable accomplishment in support of the development was the establishment of national training agencies (NTAs). Jamaica's Human Employment and Resource Training Trust / National Training Agency (HEART Trust / NTA) led the way in 1991, followed by Barbados, Trinidad and Tobago, Antigua, Bahamas, Belize, Guyana, Montserrat, and St. Lucia. The NTAs are governmental organisations with the responsibility to develop, organise, promote, and monitor a viable TVET system within each country. In pursuance, a major strategy for heightening regional development of TVET was the formation of the Caribbean Association of National Training Agencies (CANTA) in 2003. A quote from the CANTA (2013) webpage reads, 'Caribbean Community member states have long realised the importance of TVET in relation to workforce development and economic competitiveness and have made individual country-level efforts to establish their training systems' (p. 1). CANTA (2013) sees its goals as

a) to promote the development of a competitive regional workforce, and

b) to facilitate the movement of certified skilled workers within the Caribbean Single Market and Economy (CSME).

This organisation therefore serves to heighten the TVET communication within the region as the NTAs strive to support respective ministries of government in the creation of greater access to relevant and quality TVET programmes in an equitable manner.

In all this, the pace of TVET advancement within the region is far slower than it may have been, and one of the debilitating factors in this regard is seen to be the maintenance of the age-old depressing image of TVET in its earlier forms: manual training and apprenticeship during the slavery and postslavery eras. Attitudes are slow in changing, although there have been several attempts to justify TVET as a part of general education and to craft holistic policies that will include discipline at all levels in education.

3.4. TVET, Workforce, and Gender Considerations in the Caribbean

Progress in female TVET involvement within the region might have been more advanced were it not for the existence of certain challenges relating to gender considerations. According to Cooke and Baptiste (2012), from a gender perspective, the design of a TVET programme should provide for the elimination of inequalities in the delivery of knowledge, skills, and competencies among men and women. They continued that although more girls are participating in TVET now than before and are overrepresented in training institutions, on the job, they are underrepresented in science, engineering, and other traditionally male-dominated occupations, not only in participation, but also in TVET delivery. This seems an obvious spin-off from the hidden curriculum whereby, according to Chisholm (2009), controllers of the education and training systems show bias in their registration patterns: there is always limited space or often no space for females in certain TVET areas; hence, they are confined to the few traditionally female-centred areas for training.

Another challenging consideration cited by Cooke et al. (2012) is that apart from male dominance, in the first case, overrepresentation always results in a market glut or, at best, a soft market that induces low wages in the affected skill areas. In the second case, the male-dominated, 'hard' skills attract higher salaries, hence the finding that typically, women still earn 60 percent to 75 percent of males' wages and have a higher unemployment rate within the region. The sociocultural images of TVET and of women continue to hamper progress in its delivery and participation. TVET has, over decades, suffered from an image that relegates the discipline to a low position on the social ladder. Because of the historical background of TVET in the region, for an elongated period, TVET has been known to conjure up images of slavery, menial settings, hands-only engagement, dirty work, and work for the academically weak. The perception is that based on the background, girls especially are still channelled away from those areas—e.g. construction and metal/mechanical works—which are often referred to as *hard skills*. The enduring sociocultural image of women coming out of slavery and plantation society confines the group, and in some forms, albeit reduced, they are still viewed as chattel, drawers of wood and water, performers of all household chores, bearers and nurturers of children. In great measure, due to these persistent images, although in mitigated forms, Cooke et al. have been led to conclude that today, the job market still has not been gender sensitive; for example, job advertisements specify female jobs, which are mostly lower wage, and the workplace makes no provision for helping women balance domestic responsibilities.

3.5. Gender and TVET in Caribbean Schools

Problems with TVET in recent years as they relate to quality workforce preparedness within the region could have been obviated if the stage was set at the earliest level of the school system. Lauglo (2006) referred to a holistic policy whereby provision must be made for the range of beneficiaries, including all levels in school and all human groupings, that ought to be considered. It would have stymied much of the current barriers, especially if discriminating features of the hidden curriculum were uprooted, and *TVET for all* was promoted. The formalisation of vocational training in the Caribbean began from the early twentieth century and developed as TVET in schools by the middle of the same century. While this is commendable, the dawning of the twenty first century has yet to show an adequate balance, as some gender differences in terms of training still exist and have significant impact on the workplace.

A pilot was launched in Jamaica (1998–2009) to explore the integration of TVET in secondary schools' curricula. With all its effort and attributes, the Jamaican pilot did not pointedly consider creating adequate gender balance in stating its objectives. Based on the study done by Powell (2013), in terms of gender, of the eleven programmes piloted, four were gender neutral, but those that were male oriented, as dictated by the hidden curriculum, were five in number; they were auto mechanics, building construction, electrical/electronics, metalwork engineering, and plumbing. These outnumbered the two female-oriented ones: cosmetology and garment construction. This is not to say that girls and boys were deliberately barred from respective sets of programmes and not to say that there weren't the few outlier cases; however, the question of gender balancing especially by way of career counselling was never brought to the fore. Programme selection, though steered by input of programmes in career development, was not seen to veer focus from traditional views in any significant way.

The Jamaican pilot, by strategic planning and massive resource input and upgrading, sought to increase access to TVET in terms of creating opportunities, increasing participation, and facilitating transitions. In spite of efforts made to achieve the goal, however, the population within the pilot domain was seen to have had a lower-than-expected regard for the discipline. Data from the case study (2013, 229–233) show that in 2007, for example, from an enrolment total of 1,508 grade 11 students in TVET programmes, only 926 registered for TVET external examinations, and 552 passed. Thus, the rate of certification for that year was 36 percent. A closer look at passing rates for male- and female-oriented programmes for the same year shows 40 percent passed for the five male-oriented programmes and 56 percent for the two female-oriented programmes. Hence, this interpretation: if figures are to be viewed in relation to the labour market, there have been fewer males qualified or available to take up more positions. This type of situation logically leads to labour shortages, hence higher wages. On the other hand, more females have become qualified and available to take up fewer positions, a situation that logically leads to gluts, hence lower wages. This interpretation can help to explain in part the regional, if not global, phenomenon of lower wages for females in the workplace. However, figures from the pilot will not be typical for the country or for the region since the pilot provision has been made for all upper-secondary students to participate, and they have been literally herded into participation. The figures, however, give an indication as to what is more likely to be obtained within the region, where similar efforts have been made to increase access without stressing gender balancing. Though increases have been seen in some countries in the region, as encouraged by examples like the Jamaican pilot and the support of NTAs, the overall figures that show the region's reality can be more impressive and can edge closer to address MDG number 3.

UNESCO (2012), in its report on UN Economic Commission for Latin America and the Caribbean (2007), notes that 'although net enrolment rates at both primary and secondary levels have steadily increased in most countries for the past ten years for both sexes, dropout rates have also increased' (p. 1). Further, the study has found that Caribbean education systems failed to prepare young people adequately for skilled jobs for the global economy. The study claims evidence in the fact that despite eleven years of formal education, many school leavers still lack marketable skills, and hence, employability prospects have been low. Interestingly, the UNESCO report cites Caribbean youth as referring to their education experience by using such terms as boring, limited, academic-focused, and ultratraditional. This, the UNESCO writers add, has been reported by Eye on the Future, the 2010 report of the CARICOM Commission on Youth Development. The disaffection of youth with educational experiences has also been underlined in the report by its indication that especially, males underperform in education and training, which has led to overall low male participation and achievement seen at all levels of the education system. This may be attributed to some underlying factors examined, such as outdated curricula and teaching methods and limited numbers of training institutions, especially at the tertiary level. In the UNDP (2010) report, Jamaica has reported the following in 2009:

> Within the school system causes are thought to include pedagogy, the traditional bias towards academic subjects, and the social stigma still attached to skills training geared to boys, and the gender bias of some teachers exhibited in more punitive measures towards boys. (p. 16)

Due to these factors, there are resultant skills shortages in key sectors of the Caribbean economy.

The Trinidadian experience of having to outsource construction projects—i.e. outside the region—is stark proof of an existing situation of skills shortage. Franklin et al. (2009) describes Trinidad and Tobago as an energy-based Caribbean economy that earns substantial revenues from the mineral. By way of financial successes in this regard, Franklin et al. share that the country's Vision 2020 has great focus on structural reforms in support of reduction of unemployment and poverty rates. Embarking on a wave of investments in physical building is a major part of the government's strategy. Because of the inflow of foreign direct investment and increase in employment rates, the government's massive infrastructural construction and low-income housing development strategy have been paralleled by commercial and private citizens' demand for buildings, new housing, and renovations respectively. The demand for skills to satisfy the construction subsector has obviously increased. Without concomitant increase in training of persons in the special skills, labour shortages have ensued. Franklin et al. state 'One reason for the shortfall . . . is the reality of vocational education and training (VET) is currently not (and has not been for some time) producing the numbers of skilled workers for the construction sector in Trinidad and Tobago' (p. 144). Thus, in order to address the problem, Trinidad and Tobago has embarked upon the importation of skilled labour from within the region as well as contracting priority construction projects to extraregional countries such as USA, China, France, and Malaysia.

Similar regional skills shortages have been seen, for example arc welders for bauxite in Guyana and Jamaica. It is important to note, however, that in spite of the labour shortages that especially in the case of Trinidad and Tobago, present the need for higher-than-normal labour cost of international proportions, engaging local women in skills training from the level of the school and beyond for these sectors, in order to benefit from greater numbers, has not been substantially introduced as an option, although there is high female unemployment in these countries.

3.6. Women Empowerment in the Caribbean

In order to adequately explore the advancement in empowerment of Caribbean women, it is, at this juncture, very important to examine the meaning of the term *empowerment*, followed by a justification of its desirability, especially in the case of women. Page and Czuba (1999), in attesting to the multidimensional nature of the term, describe empowerment as a process that disposes persons to master the controls over their lives. They continue that this process also fosters power in persons for use in their communities and their society as they deem it fit and important. Hence, in order for the process to progress, opportunities must be created, resources made available, skills and knowledge imparted to individuals for their motivation to strategize towards self-improvement. Thus, empowerment is not an endowment, but given the required support in terms of opportunities and resources, it has to be achieved by the self for the self and the group or the community. There are therefore sociological and psychological dimensions that in the end have implications for a dimension that is economic. Due to the all-embracing nature of TVET, broadening and increasing access is a sure way of addressing all these dimensions and ensuring empowerment.

Empowerment of women in the region is on the increase as the facilitation of gender equality is so permitting in terms of access to education and training. The three pillars necessary for attaining gender equality as identified by UNDP researchers (2010) are economic independence, physical autonomy, and participation in decision-making. Thus, implicit in the meaning ascribed to empowerment, these are the same indices by which empowerment of women may be measured. For reemphasis, most contributions in a UNESCO-UNEVOC online conference aver that the relationship between women and TVET is affected by political, social, and economic measures and not confined to directly enforceable measures by TVET alone. They have found that these measures are necessary to reduce or eliminate barriers in enabling equal access for women in TVET. In spite of these points of awareness and efforts made, it has been noted that for developing countries like these in the Caribbean, although the empowerment process for women is in action, it has been slow. There have been some regional successes in this regard, however; for example, in Jamaica, according to UNDP (2010) country report, the share of women in wage employment in the non-agricultural sector has risen from 37 percent in 2000 to 48.9 percent in 2007 (STATIN 2007), and there have been some important leadership positions held by women, such as prime minister, director of public prosecution, and chief justice, among others. In addition, women account for 54 percent of the permanent secretaries in ministries of the government and are now heading prominent private sector concerns, such as banks and nonbank financial entities. Some have been elected to lead prominent manufacturing and employers' groups. Significantly, employment for young women has increased in the services sector, especially tourism, call centres, and data processing. In the same UNDP report, Barbados has reported that in 2007, approximately 50 percent of managers, senior officials, and legislators as well as professional and technical workers have been women. While involvement in TVET may not be a leading factor that causes the increase in placement of women in the mentioned senior positions, it is to be noted that TVET has played an important role in preparing young women to fill services sector positions.

According to the UNDP report (2010), in the region, empowerment seems to fail in the area of violence against women, and the percentage of women holding seats in parliament is still low; the highest reported is 29 percent in Guyana, while in 2006, St. Kitts has reported no women in the national parliament. In furtherance, UNDP has made the following statement: 'Despite the strides made by women in education and their increasing numbers in administrative and managerial positions, there is still the cultural mindset which continues to insist that women's roles must be secondary to men' (p. 30) In response to this troubling condition, governments' provision of equitable access to TVET for men and women, with concomitant access to job opportunities, will be the best bet. The sense of self that being skilled entails (independence, self-assurance, and creativity) can create a culture change, and women will be more willing and capable to lead.

In order to analyze Caribbean achievements relative to MDG 3, a comparative look at the situation as obtained in prominent first-world countries will be of use.

3.7. MDG Number 3, TVET, and Developed Countries

In examining the MGDs, it is important to observe that most of the goals are targeted towards developing and underdeveloped countries, since they address matters that can be treated mainly by economic input. Goal number 3 can however, be said to be targeted towards developed, developing, and underdeveloped countries since it speaks largely to issues of a fundamentally cultural rather than economic nature. Hence, the way in which the goal is addressed in developed countries with a robust TVET base can be instructive. New Zealand and the United Kingdom are the two developed countries selected.

New Zealand boasts one of the most highly recognised education systems in the world and is reported to emphasise TVET in high schools as well as in colleges. According to a report on training by New Zealand College (2013), 'the education ministry has taken up proactive measures to ensure that this form of education supports sustainable development in the nature-enriched country' (p. 1). With this in view, special care has been taken for women to receive good careers by ensuring their involvement in the discipline. This is against the backdrop of a gender parity index in the ratio of girls to boys, of 1.00 in primary level enrolment, 1.05 in secondary, and 1.46 in tertiary as recently as 2010. This information has been retrieved in the country level data for MDG indicators.

In terms of women empowerment in New Zealand, care has been taken to support this aspect largely through the Art of Living Foundation's (2013) programmes, which claim thus:

> Provide a solid foundation that nurtures the inner strength, creativity and self-esteem of women from all walks of life. With this base established well, women are able to go out into the world, prepared to handle any challenge with skills, confidence and grace. They come to the forefront, where they become agents of peace and positive social change for themselves, their families, other women and their society. (p. 1)

MDG indicators show that in 2011, the share of women in wage employment in non-agricultural sector is 50.2% percent, and the proportion of seats held by women in national parliament in 2013 is 32.2 percent.

The United Kingdom has also been reported as having a robust education system, with TVET as a beacon in its curriculum for both genders. In putting skills at the heart of global economic success, the British Council (2012) states thus:

Vocational education and training is the key to developing the skilled and motivated workforce needed to maintain workplace standards, boost commercial success and promote social cohesion. The UK is committed to skills development, and invests more than £60 billion on technical, vocational education and training each year. This has enabled the UK to develop an educational system that is internationally recognized for its high quality standards and its success in delivering the knowledge and skills that employers need to remain competitive and ensure a brighter economic future. (p ii)

In respect of MDG number 3, statistics for the UK show that in terms of gender parity, the ratio of girls to boys in primary education in 2010 is 0.99; at secondary level, it is 1.01, and at tertiary, 1.38. The 2011 figure for share of women in wage employment in the nonagricultural sector is 46.7percent, and the proportion of seats held by women in national parliament in 2013 is 22.5 percent.

3.8. Comparative Analysis

Both New Zealand and the UK present a similar background in terms of the strength of their respective educational systems, which emphasise TVET as an imperative in placing their countries at the zenith of relative economic success. The extent to which this status has separated them from the Caribbean in addressing MDG number 3 may be analyzed in reference to table 3.1 which speaks to gender equality specifically in access to education, and table 3.2 which speaks to empowerment of women via level of wage employment and representation in national political leadership. Bearing in mind the question posed by the title of this paper as to whether or not TVET and its salient contribution to WFD is best positioned to address goal number 3, the comparative tables will serve to support the analysis. A selection of the four leading Caribbean countries in terms of their involvement with TVET and membership in CANTA will be represented in the comparison; these are Barbados, Guyana, Jamaica, and Trinidad and Tobago.

Table 3.1. Gender Parity Index: Ratio of Girls to Boys

Education Level	Year	NZ	UK	B'DOS	GUY	JAM	T&T
Primary	2010	1.00	0.99	1.02	1.04	0.95	0.97
	2000	1.00	1.00	1.05	0.96	0.99	0.99
Secondary	2010	1.05	1.01	1.09	1.11	1.03	1.07 (2008)
	2000	1.06	1.01	1.11	1.01 (2001)	1.02	1.10
Tertiary	2010	1.46	1.38	2.38	2.52	2.29 (2009)	1.28 (2005)
	2000	1.46	1.19	2.85	1.84 (2004)	1.82	1.48

Key:

NZ - New Zealand

UK - United Kingdom

B'DOS - Barbados

GUY - Guyana

JAM - Jamaica

T&T - Trinidad & Tobago

In table 3.1, the figures for primary and secondary enrolment infer three major findings:

1. There are no significant differences between the developed countries earmarked and the highlighted Caribbean countries, as they relate to enrolment by gender.

2. No major changes have been seen from baseline to current figures.

3. The figures in general show gender parity over the years under scrutiny.

For tertiary enrolment, table 3.1 indicates that

i. enrolment in the developed countries has remained steady over the years, with slight increases in girls' enrolment over boys.

ii. except for Trinidad and Tobago, where female enrolment far outstrips that of males, greater than 2:1, implying significant gender imbalance against males.

Whereas it has been explicitly stated by New Zealand and the UK that special effort is made to involve females equitably in TVET, it should not be assumed that the same strategy is obtained in the Caribbean. Hence, although MDG number 3 in terms of schooling seems to be equally addressed in the Caribbean, one may well conclude that the downfall exists within the region because of a lack in the will to ensure equity in access to TVET, which can be beneficial in terms of being a strategy for economic development.

Table 3.2. Empowerment of *Women:*
Employment and Political Representation

Indicator	Year	NZ	UK	B'DOS	GUY	JAM	T&T
Percentage of women in wage employment in the nonagricultural sector	2001	50.2	46.7	50.7 (2008)	37.0 (2002)	48.2 (2008)	46.3 (2010)
	2000	49.8	46.0	49.9	38.7 (1997)	45.0	40.0
Percentage of seats held by women in national parliament	2013	32.2	22.0	10.0	31.3	12.7	28.6
	2000	29.2	18.4	10.7	18.5	13.3	11.1

Key:

NZ - 	New Zealand

UK - 	United Kingdom

B'DOS - Barbados

GUY - 	Guyana

JAM - 	Jamaica

T&T - 	Trinidad & Tobago

Based on the figures displayed in table 3.2, there are two major findings:

1. In terms of nonagricultural wage employment, apart from Guyana, female employment has retained status of near parity in the developed as well as Caribbean countries over the years under review.

2. The proportion of seats held in national parliament in both sets of countries remains low.

The UN statistics division from whence the data for tables 3.1 and 3.2 have come implies that indicators that speak to

MDG number 3 reside in education, employment, and national political leadership. The comparative display on education shows that developed countries are far less erratic in terms of school enrolment practices, as they have been able so far, to maintain gender balance in this regard. The Caribbean countries, for the most part, have moved to an extreme 2:1 imbalance in favour of females at the tertiary level. In terms of empowerment, one will imagine that tertiary-level involvement plays a role just as well as will employment and opportunities to participate in national leadership at the parliamentary level. The observation is that in spite of strategies for a full-fledged education system that pointedly stresses access to TVET, with special emphasis on inclusion of women, this has not translated into widespread demonstration of empowerment as measured by their involvement in national politics. We are yet to see where personal empowerment of women based on other measures shows more encouraging results. According to Bartlay (2013), 'figures suggest that women only currently make up 17% of business-owners in the UK and are half as likely as their male counterparts to start a new business venture, signifying a need to offer more female entrepreneur role models' (p. 1) Bartlay continues, 'We must see more representation of the female entrepreneur who has set up an engineering company, the female CIO, the female welder or the female manufacturing business owner'. The obvious preoccupation here is female empowerment, which seems to be progressing at a slow rate. From Canada, another developed country, the Canadian government (2013), speaking of MDG number 3, has shared the following sentiment:

> Millennium Development Goal (MDG) 3, the promotion of gender equality and women's empowerment, is the only MDG that is both a goal in itself and recognized as essential to the achievement of all the other Millennium Development Goals. An educated mother, for

example, can have a positive effect on her child's educational opportunities. What's more, enhancing women's access to credit and finance, as well as their ability to inherit or own land, can unlock the untapped potential of women entrepreneurs. (p. 1)

In other words, the educated mother will be fully prepared with TVET as a critical part of her education. Personal empowerment will be achieved if TVET forms a part of her proverbial artillery because TVET ensures the application of knowledge, access; therefore, credit, finance, and all other such resources will be maximised to be of utmost benefit to the family, community, and society when she applies knowledge gained and puts each unit of resource through the productive process.

Comparatively speaking, figures-measuring levels of addressing MDG number 3, as seen in tables 3.1 and 3.2, hardly show differences of any significance between the developed countries and the Caribbean. However, there is stability implied by figures of the developed countries, especially in tertiary enrolment, over the years. The facts on low unemployment rates for 2014 (6 percent in UK, 5.4 percent in NZ) and persistent high GDP per capita ($37,500 in UK, $35,374 in NZ) show how their integration of TVET throughout the system may have contributed to development in these countries. In the case of the Caribbean, where there is little integration of TVET, unemployment rates typically, in 2014, range between 11 percent in Guyana and a high of 15.03 percent in Jamaica, with GDP being $8,000 and $9,100 respectively. Here, the extreme changes as seen in tertiary-level enrolment indicate an imbalance that may well be TVET-related. It has been mooted that especially, males' underperformance and underenrolment may be attributed to the straight academic nature of curricula, accompanied by traditional methodology in teaching as well as among other things, a lack in training opportunities especially at the tertiary level.

For MDG number 3, differences in empowerment levels as measured by employment and political representations are not seen to be of much significance between both sets of countries on average. TVET does not seem to influence output in this regard neither for one set nor for the other. Cultural retentions and philosophical underpinnings seem to be of greater influence. However, the developed countries with rich CTVET tapestry definitely show the existence of more equipped women in wage employment, thus adding to the countries' economic success. This is as opposed to Caribbean countries that have need to import skills or do without, to their own economic demise.

3.9. Recommendations for the Caribbean

3.9.1. Holistic Policy Development and Implementation:

A review of the system of education in New Zealand and the UK shows gender parity at all rungs of the education ladder and an enduring effort to place TVET at the centre for social maturity and economic development. This is clear evidence of the existence of a holistic policy for TVET that sees to inclusion of TVET at all education levels and for both genders, from kinder through primary and secondary to tertiary and university. Caribbean countries need to examine this strategy for emulation, especially since they have, over the years, through NTAs, gathered enough momentum to develop these policies for TVET and implement them. The promulgation and implementation of a policy for TVET should follow closely on the heels of its development for early effectiveness.

3.9.2. Increase Access to TVET

The developed countries have demonstrated in great measure participation in the three strands of access to TVET. The strands are access as opportunities, access as participation, and access as transition. Access as opportunities focuses on clearing physical, social, and psychological barriers to TVET. Whereas clearance of physical and social barriers has obviously been achieved in these countries, clearance of some psychological barriers seems to be in abeyance because figures for empowerment of women remain low. For the Caribbean to achieve access as opportunities to any desired extent, in terms of physical barriers, the strategy to upgrade and share TVET resources on a phased basis, as piloted in Jamaica, is a cost-effective measure and should be implemented. In terms of seeking to clear social and psychological barriers, however, strong public awareness, career guidance and counselling, and mentoring programmes should be engaged. These measures should be geared at eliminating traditional views on the status of women, the status of TVET, and how society can benefit from their full inclusion.

Access as participation focuses on increasing and broadening the TVET learner base to amply satisfy the workforce. Developed countries, much like Caribbean countries, have exhibited gender parity in respect of schooling (see table 3.1). However, based on their philosophy of TVET and WFD, the women of these developed countries will have significantly more exposure to the discipline than those in the Caribbean. Thus, there is a broader learner base for TVET than that in the Caribbean to adequately satisfy the workforce. The access as participation strand may also be measured by the unemployment index, which for the UK is 6.3 percent and New Zealand 5.4 percent, both in 2014. They have accomplished a great deal in this area when compared with Caribbean lands, such as Guyana showing 11.1 percent, Barbados showing 13.2 percent and Jamaica showing 15.3 percent all during the same year, 2014. The outlier case, Trinidad and Tobago showing 3.8 percent, could not have achieved this status due to benefits from involvement in TVET but largely based on their labour importation experiences already discussed. It may be argued that it is owing to their current endowment via buoyancy in the price of crude oil (Franklin and Hosein 2009) that hefty injections of finance capital have induced a flurry of other employment activities. A focus on increasing the pool of learners in TVET by expanding the offerings of all programmes to both males and females in the Caribbean will see to adequacy in the number of skilled personnel for the workforce and will better address MDG number 3.

Access as transition focuses on articulation within TVET tracks and, importantly, articulation to professions and the job market. Whereas women in the developed countries continue to benefit from this strand of access to TVET, in the region, the benefits remain at a low. This obtains mainly because the Caribbean people have stuck to traditional biases that ascribe a low image to the discipline and have so far failed to fully integrate it into curricula. If TVET is rightfully marketed as an element of general education and engaged in by all students at the various levels of the system, it will become acceptable to all. Access, therefore, in all strands will be facilitated rather than be continually sidestepped. Unemployment and underemployment rates will fall, and also, the need to import expertise for highly specialised tasks will be reduced or eliminated because well-prepared women will fill the gaps.

3.9.3. Develop, Strengthen, and Maintain Public-Private Partnerships:

This strategy has accounted for much of the successes yielded in New Zealand and the UK; however, if there is a higher level of female empowerment, more women will be involved in these partnerships, and enriched decision-making will take place at higher levels. The Caribbean will greatly benefit from enhanced standards of living should female empowerment be improved by strengthening the participation of women in private-public partnerships.

3.10. Conclusion

MDG number 3 points to the heart of harmonious family development and the overall enhancement of human well-being. If the young is schooled, they become enabled to lead productive and independent lives. If in school they are led to become cognizant of the importance of all others in cohort in spite of gender and are made to value themselves, then in adult life, they will exhibit a high level of gender awareness, tolerance, and self-worth. All these lead to personal empowerment. However, the nature of and content in curricula is important in concretizing the desirable student outcomes, after which the workforce hankers. CTVET has been said to be many things, especially in respect of its value as a learned discipline to the development of the modern workforce. It is thus imperative for human and economic development and must be pursued in support of addressing any goal to develop human capital, improve infrastructure, and increase social, economic, and political rights in aid of the enhancement of basic standard of living.

The focus of the paper is on MDG number 3. A comparative look at the region against selected world powers shows little difference in achievement when measured in terms of gender parity in educational enrolments, share of female in nonagricultural employment, and proportion of national parliamentary participation. The statistics, however, do not cover standard of living of families, but the results of that index may be translated into economic well-being per capita. This is decidedly high in the two developed countries, which are not only exemplars in education systems worldwide, but also, they employ CTVET as an imperative. Should the Caribbean region desire to 'try their hands' at becoming economically successful, it will be instructive for them to add the missing element TVET as an integral part of all curricula. It will also be instructive to avoid the hidden curriculum that gears the system to steer females away from participation in vital CTVET programmes that are necessary for the workforce, as in these areas, there always exist shortages on competent manpower, leading sometimes to importation of labour.

Any attempt to address MDG number 3 is an effort to unlock the untapped potential of women. Inclusion of CTVET in this effort will see to real and valued changes in the utilisation of resources, be it human, physical, or material. The Caribbean will do well to be advised by countries like New Zealand and the UK, as they place skills at the heart of global economic success. Although besieged by CTVET-related challenges, regional governments, guided by the Caribbean Association of National Training Agencies (CANTA), should study the systems of developed countries in order to emulate their best practices in this regard.

3.11. References

Barltay, B. 2013. 'Call to Increase Numbers of Women Business Leaders'. The HR Director. Retrieved http://www.hrdirector.com/business-news/diversity_and_equality/call-to-increase.

British Council. 2012. 'Putting Skills at the Heart of Global Economic Success: A Brief Guide to UK Technical, Vocational Education and Training (TVET)'.

Canadian Government. 2013. 'Promote Gender Equality and Empower Women: Overview'. *Foreign Affairs, Trade and Development Canada*. Retrieved http://www.acdi-cida.gc.ca/acdi-cida.nsf/eng/JUD-131841-HC7.

Caribbean Association of National Training Agencies (CANTA). 2013. Retrieved http://cantaonline.org/.

CARICOM Commission on Youth Development. 2010. 'Eye on the Future: Investing in Youth Now for Tomorrow's Community'. CARICOM Secretariat, Guyana.

Cooke, L., and E. Baptiste. 2012. 'Challenges of Integrating Gender Considerations in TVET in the Caribbean'. Presented at Caribbean Conference on TVET, Montego Bay, Jamaica, March 7–9.

Franklin, M., and R. Hosein. 2009. 'Coping with Labor Shortages in the Construction Sector of Trinidad and Tobago with Emphasis on VET'. *Caribbean Journal of Education* 1 (31), April.

Gregory, R. 2003. 'The Role of TVET and the Caribbean Association of National Training Agencies (CANTA) and Allied Bodies within the Caribbean Single Market and Economy (CSME)'. Retrieved www.docstoc.com/docs/34964894.

Giloth, R. 2000. 'Learning from the Field: Economic Growth and Workforce Development in the 1990s'. *Economic Development Quarterly* 14 (4), Sage.

Ki-Moon, B. 2010. Foreword in the United Nations Millennium Development Goals Report.

Lauglo, J. 2006. 'Research for TVET Policy Development.' UNEVOC International Centre for TVET.

Morris, H. 2009. 'Developing Policies for Technical Vocational Education and Training (TVET) in the Caribbean'. *Caribbean Journal of Education* 31 (1), special issue on mainstreaming TVET in the Caribbean.

National Centre for Education and Training for Addiction (NCETA). 2002. 'What Is Workforce Development?' National Research Centre of Australia on Alcohol and Other Drugs Workforce Development, Flinders University.

New Zealand College. 2013. 'Training New Zealand.' Retrieved [www.new-zealand-college.com/training-new-zealand/1286/.

Page, N., and C. Czuba. 1999. 'Empowerment: What Is It?' *Extension Journal Inc.*, ISSN 1077-5315.

Powell, C. 2013. 'Towards a Model for Engaging the Jamaican Secondary Schools in Efficient Delivery of TVET'. Unpublished thesis, University of the West Indies, Mona, Jamaica, West Indies.

The Art of Living. 2013. 'Women Empowerment: Empowering Women Socially and Economically'. The Art of Living Foundation, New Zealand.

UNDP. 2010. 'Achieving the Millennium Development Goals with Equality in Latin America and the Caribbean: Progress and Challenges'.

UNESCO. 2001. 'Revised Recommendation Concerning Technical and Vocational Education in Normative Instruments Concerning Technical and Vocational Education'.

_____. 2012. 'Skills Training in the Caribbean: An Eye on the Future'.

UNESCO-UNIVOC. 2011. 'Women and TVET.' Online conference report, December 5–15.

United Nations. 2013. 'We Can End Poverty: Millennium Development Goals and Beyond 2015 Fact Sheet'. Retrieved www.un.org/millenniumgoals/pdf/goal_3_fs.pdf.

UN Statistics Division. 2013. 'Millennium Development Goals Indicators'. Retrieved http://mdgs.un.org/unsd/mdg/Data.aspx.

World Bank. 2012. 'Gender Equality and Development'. World Development Report.

World Development Report. 2012. 'Gender Differences in Employment and Why They Matter'. Chapter 5, pp. 198–253.

CHAPTER 4

Quality Assurance: An Exploration of Its Benefits in the Management of Twenty-First-Century CTVET in Caribbean Secondary Schools

Elaine Shakes

Secondary education is that fundamental conduit between the primary and tertiary stages in the educational hierarchy; its purviews are the preparation of students for higher education and the world of work. A part of the global renewed prominence of Career, technical and vocational education and training (CTVET) is its recognition as the most profound strategy to accomplish and sustain the human capital in the twenty-first century, to achieve Education for All (EFA) and United Nations Millennium Development Goals (MDGs). Globalisation is one of the critical influences impacting the reforms of CTVET outcomes, delivery, assessment, certification, and employment. Consequently, there is consensus in the Caribbean education communities regarding the relevance of secondary schools, that competencies developed in the secondary education system must match the requirements of the economy and labour force by laying the foundation for students' entry into productive work and lifelong learning. Without this foundation, a person faces difficulties gaining and maintaining a job that requires ongoing learning to adapt to new technologies, new products and services, and new forms of organisations.

These new CTVET obligations have created a novel set of relationships among education, employment, and the labour market. Inevitably, a shift from the traditional secondary schools' negative perception of technical vocational education and training (TVET) and the current methods used to place students in these areas are urgent imperatives. The holistic educational development aimed for by Caribbean secondary schools must encompass a merger of TVET and general education to enable beneficiaries to master information and skills relevant to the standards required for the region's industrialisation, competeviness, and economic and social prosperity.

Standards are driving the competitiveness and criteria for quality in the production of goods and the provision of services in economic activities and are now being demanded from the education system by stakeholders. Central, therefore, to TVET operational reforms in Caribbean secondary schools are the adoption of a system of agreed standards, total quality management, and recognition driven by stakeholders to empower institutions to adapt and respond appropriately to the socio-economic milieu. Sustainable capacity building (curricula and occupational standards; workshops/laboratories; classroom designs; instructions for cognitive, metacognitive, and psychomotor skills; teacher training and development) and financing of supporting systems and structures are fundamental to the satisfactory achievement of the standards required for the region's human capacity development and workforce relevance.

It is incumbent on stakeholders, the main beneficiaries of TVET, to be intimately involved at all levels of TVET reforms in secondary education. Stakeholders must, of necessity, position themselves as key owners and regulators of TVET's inputs, processes, and outputs in collaboration with the ministries of education, secondary school management and staff, and the Caribbean Examinations Council.

The Caribbean secondary TVET programmes are examined and certified by the Caribbean Examinations Council (CXC). CXC is the regional examining body that provides examinations for secondary and post-secondary candidates in Caribbean countries. The vision of CXC is to ensure the global intellectual competitiveness of the Caribbean through the provision of quality assurance in education and comprehensive certification. CXC has launched several initiatives aimed at defining new directions in technical education and rationalizing the certification that it offers in that domain. Among the council's goals is to get TVET *right* at the secondary level.

TVET is now an indisputably huge socio-economic system, requiring all beneficiaries (government, education, industry, businesses, and communities) to create collaborative, innovative, and quality support systems, structures, and policies without which the new TVET vision and mission cannot be effectively accomplished. An all-inclusive approach, therefore, in the achievement of quality to radically reform secondary school TVET must be pursued by the Caribbean Examinations Council. The major readjustments must be embedded in the development of a mutual system for a shared understanding of quality assurance, the development of and implementation of differentiated delivery, assessment, and placement approaches (on-the-job training, job shadowing, and apprenticeship) capable of meeting the needs of every learner and satisfying the foundational requirements of national, regional, and international labour markets.

This chapter focuses attention on CXC's quality assurance of the TVET programmes offered in Caribbean secondary schools. The primary element explores the benefits of a demand-led quality assurance conceptual framework that which is designed to strengthen the participation and collaboration of governments, stakeholders, and the social partners in creating a culture of quality in the management of twenty-first-century TVET programmes in Caribbean secondary schools.

It is the expectation that this conceptual framework will be ratified with further consultations with all TVET entities, professionals, practitioners, and stakeholders in the Caribbean. These are critical to the development of the inconclusive areas of the framework—for example, the development of the criteria and rating system and other tools desired for the effective use of the demand-led quality assurance framework. Additionally, it is the expectation that this chapter will contribute to the existing body of knowledge, principles, and procedures in quality assurance. Throughout this chapter, it is understood that the term TVET includes career education and is used interchangeably with CTVET.

4.1. Introduction

UNESCO-UNEVOC (2008) purports that the development of an effective technical and vocational education and training (TVET) system is at the heart of education reform efforts. Secondary general education, work-related knowledge, and skills have the potential at the foundation level to enable students to understand TVET, to increase access to TVET, to ensure that students develop productivity and work skills consistent with industry standards, and to enable them to obtain recognised and marketable credentials for integration in the workforce. The response to these TVET significances will require a high level of sustainable human resource base, systems, structures, and operational mechanisms to deliver and assess the competencies and to ensure their compatibility with labour market pathways and lifelong learning.

According to Bennell (1999), the role of TVET in furnishing skills required to improve productivity, raise income levels, and improve access to employment opportunities has been widely recognised.

In support of Bennell, Nyerere (2009) asserts that developments in the last three decades have made the role of TVET more decisive in the globalisation process, technological change, and increased competition due to trade liberalisation. These developments have also necessitated the requirements for higher skills and productivity among workers in modern sector firms, micro and small enterprises.

Joel (2006) posits that in the nineteenth century, countries that have mastered chemistry and physics of the day and have put materials to work by means of the industrial revolution have been at the leading edge of the world's economy. In the twentieth century, countries that have mastered energy principally from fossil fuel, oil, and natural gas and have put energy to work have been at the leading edge of the world's economy. We are currently living with the consequences and problems of the nineteenth and twentieth century. In the twenty-first century, countries that will be at the leading edge of the world's economy will be those whose people will best master information and put that mastery to work. The current focus is increasingly upon preparing knowledge workers to meet the challenges posed during the transitions from the industrial to the information age.

It is incumbent on secondary-level TVET to provide the enabling opportunities for the development of the calibre of engineers, technicians, technical managers, and professionals required by the knowledge-based global economy. Learners must acquire and demonstrate competencies and skills with greater understanding and application of technology, multiple literacy, and critical thinking. Such learners should also be adaptable, highly employable, and possess the skills to undertake technologically driven careers.

The United Nations Decade of Education for Sustainable Development (DESD 2005–2014) refers to quality TVET for a sustainable future and links education and training with economic and social policies. Education, training, and lifelong learning are fundamental and should form an integral part of and be consistent with the comprehensive economic, fiscal, social, and labour market policies and programmes that are vital for sustainable economic growth, employment creation (decent work), and social development. The success of the goals of education for sustainable development is dependent on the network and alliances that will develop among stakeholders at all levels.

The UNESCO education strategy (2008) perceives work-related knowledge and skills in general secondary education as desirable in helping it to be reoriented to better equip young people with competencies for life. Consequently, the development, application, and sustainability of these competencies within secondary education are compelling TVET administrators, practitioners, facilitators, and professionals to work collaboratively with stakeholders and social partners.

According to the Caribbean Association of Industry and Commerce (CAIC) (2006), under Universal Secondary Education (USE), mastery of basic cognitive skills is the basis for a productive human resource base and the gateway to further professional education. The association gives support to the goals of USE and reiterates that its success will be determined by its relevance to labour market demands.

The CARICOM Secretariat (2008) postulates that one of the main pillars of the Caribbean Single Market and Economy (CSME) is the free movement of skilled persons throughout the region. The issues of skill development through TVET and the portability of qualifications have assumed renewed importance in positioning the region for competitive participation in the new economy. In order to achieve this, there must be a common system and understanding of quality assurance issues at all levels of education and training, including TVET.

The recognition in the region of standards through quality assurance in education for the improvement of employability and competitiveness, the development of service economies, the concept of self-sufficiency, and the introduction of the Caribbean Vocational Qualification (CVQ) in the secondary system has placed substantial pressures on the Caribbean Examinations Council to rethink its approach in its TVET offerings and certification.

According to Jules (2009), the current status of TVET in the secondary system and the society is perceived negatively. Low-performing students are placed in TVET areas, hence limiting the potential of these areas to respond effectively to a competitive labour force development. In 2011, Jules outlined the Caribbean Examinations Council's proposals for reinvigorating TVET. The proposals include five TVET fundamental initiatives, which are outlined below:

1. Revision of the qualifications framework to better accommodate the concept of a seamless education system, outlining multiple pathways to success in a context of continuous education.

2. Assertion of the ideal Caribbean person and the UNESCO pillars of learning as the foundational bedrock of our educational intent.

3. Articulation between different levels and types of qualification in a modular format that creates new synergies in TVET (for example, the use of CVQ level 1 for school-based assessment purposes in CSEC TVET subjects).

4. Recognition of the critical importance of effective training of TVET teachers alongside the potential role of industry experts in adding relevance and application to real-world requirements.

5. Adoption of competency-based assessment to measure the precise knowledge, skills, and behaviours that students are expected to master.

The CXC draft policy on TVET (2013) is included in the instruments aimed at accomplishing these initiatives. It is a coordinated effort by all stakeholders to guide the diversification and streamlining of TVET in the region's secondary schools.

TVET is now an indisputably huge socio-economic system, requiring all beneficiaries (government, education, industry, businesses, and communities) to create collaborative, innovative, and quality support systems, structures, and policies without which the new TVET vision and mission cannot be effectively accomplished.

The foregoing presentation impacts my personal involvement and experience in quality assurance in the CVQ at the secondary level in the Caribbean and offers a new opportunity to re-evaluate the current processes in light of the new twenty-first-century TVET emphases. This chapter focuses attention on the CXC's quality assurance of the TVET programmes offered in Caribbean secondary schools. The primary element explores the benefits of a demand-led quality assurance conceptual framework, a new quality pathway, to strengthen the participation and collaboration of governments, stakeholders, and the social partners in creating a culture of quality in the management of twenty-first-century TVET programmes in Caribbean secondary schools.

4.2. Definitions of TVET

According to UNESCO/ILO (2001), TVET is a comprehensive term referring to those aspects of the educational process, involving, in addition to general education, the study of technologies and related sciences and the acquisition of practical skills, attitudes, understanding, and knowledge relating to occupations in various sectors of economic and social lives.

UNESCO/ILO recommendations on TVET for the twenty-first century (2001) understands TVET as

- an integral part of general education;

- a means of preparing for occupational fields and for effective participation in the world of work;

- an aspect of lifelong learning and a preparation for responsible citizenship;

- a method of facilitating poverty alleviation; and

- an instrument for promoting environmentally sound, sustainable development.

Lauglo (2006) refers to TVET as deliberate interventions to bring about learning that will make people more productive (or simply adequately productive) in designated areas of economic activity (economic sectors, occupations, specific work tasks). TVET, however, will also have other purposes that are not unique to TVET and that apply to other forms of education—for example, knowledge, skills, insights, and mindsets. These are deemed to be generally valuable for the learners.

4.3. A Study of Quality Assurance in Secondary Education

4.3.1. Types of TVET Programmes in Caribbean Secondary Education

TVET programmes are planned technical, vocational, and academic teaching and training experiences that are acquired by learners. Shakes (2013) postulates that the competencies (knowledge, skills, and attitudes) are required for optimum work performance and lifelong learning essential for satisfying effectively current and emerging demands of the labour market. The competencies are delivered and assessed through a series of practical and theoretical value-added learning experiences by competent facilitators and master craftsmen working in partnership with industries and enterprises in formal, non-formal, and informal institutional settings.

4.3.2. The TVET Programmes Certified by the Caribbean Examinations Council

The programmes are the following:

- Caribbean Secondary Education Certificate (CSEC);

- Caribbean Advanced Proficiency Examination (CAPE);

- Levels 1 and 2 Caribbean Vocational Qualification.

i. The Caribbean Secondary Education Certificate

According to the 2009–2014 revised draft CSEC technical syllabuses, the TVET programmes are located in the following syllabuses:

- The industrial technology syllabuses contain the electrical and electronic technology, building and furniture technology, and mechanical engineering technology programmes. The syllabuses are a qualitative response by the Caribbean Examinations Council to the technical and vocational education and training (TVET) needs, which are relevant to manufacturing and industrialisation in the Caribbean region. The cognitive, psychomotor, and affective outcomes aimed for in the syllabuses are geared at equipping students with a solid technical foundation for lifelong learning and to enable the students to matriculate seamlessly into entry-level occupations in a wide variety of careers and post-secondary institutions.

- The family and consumer sciences syllabus (the new name proposed for the home economics syllabus) contains the family and resource management; diet, nutrition, and health; and textiles, fashion, and clothing programmes. Family and consumer sciences is an interdisciplinary career and technical field of study that deals with family well-being, human development and services, human environments, and their interrelationships. It is concerned with the development of life skills and knowledge that help people make informed decisions about well-being, relationships, and resources. The disciplines combine competencies and experiences that are responsive to demographic, socio-economic changes, and advances in science and technology necessary for transition into post-secondary education and in the family and consumer sciences work and career clusters.

- The technical drawing syllabus contains the areas of geometrical construction (plane geometry), geometrical construction (solid geometry), building drawing, and mechanical engineering drawing. The syllabus focuses on the development of competencies in geometric construction, descriptive geometry, engineering designs and graphics, and electrical, mechanical, manufacturing, and construction drafting. These skills are useful for careers in drafting, architecture, surveying, civil engineering, interior designing, design engineering, and the general construction and manufacturing industries. In addition, the programme of studies in the syllabus caters for those students who will seek entry-level employment in related fields.

ii. Caribbean Advanced Proficiency Examination (CAPE)

The Caribbean Advanced Proficiency Examination (CAPE) is designed to provide certification of the academic, vocational, and technical achievement of students in the Caribbean who, having completed a minimum of five years of secondary education, wish to further their studies. The examinations address the skills and knowledge acquired by students under a flexible and articulated system where subjects are organised in one-unit or two-unit courses, with each unit containing three modules. The 2009–2014 revised syllabuses are as follows:

- Building and mechanical engineering drawing;

- Electrical and electronics engineering technology;

- Food and nutrition.

One of the major changes in the revised draft technical syllabuses relates to the school-based assessments (SBAs). The SBAs will no longer be solely project-based. They will employ the principles of a competency-based education, training, and assessment (CBETA) through the integration of the Caribbean Vocational Qualification (CVQ) into the SBAs. This integration is aimed at making the knowledge, skills, and attitudes aimed for in the syllabuses more practical and using them as a tool for demonstrating real-world competencies. A solid educational background (academic and technical) is expected to be achieved through practical and project-based learning, designing, production, and entrepreneurial processes. In this new approach, the CSEC technical subjects will comprise successful completion of relevant level-1 CVQ units of competence, exhibited with other evidences in a school-based assessment portfolio. Regarding the CAPE revised draft technical syllabuses, the school-based assessment components will comprise a relevant level-2 unit of competence Caribbean Vocational Qualification (CVQ) for unit 1 and a full CVQ certification for unit 2. The CVQ awards will be exhibited, among other evidences, in the school-based assessment portfolio. This new initiative makes it possible for every student sitting in the examinations to exit with dual certification. Candidates who successfully complete the CSEC examinations will be awarded the CSEC certificates and a CVQ unit of competence award. Conversely, candidates who successfully complete the CAPE examinations will be awarded CAPE certificates, units of competence, and full certificates in the CVQ.

The broad range of interdisciplinary competencies aimed for in the revised draft syllabuses will contribute to the development of the attributes of the ideal Caribbean person, as documented in the 2000 Caribbean education strategy. In addition, the syllabuses will integrate all forms and levels of the education process, which will contribute to the development of all the UNESCO pillars of learning.

iii. Levels 1 and 2 Caribbean Vocational Qualification

According to the *Caribbean Examiner* (2011), the Caribbean Vocational Qualification is an award that represents the achievement of a set of competencies. These competencies define the core work practices of an occupational area consistent with the levels within the regional qualifications framework (RQF). In an effort to remain competitive within the Caribbean Single Market and Economy (CSME), a number of CARICOM states have subscribed to the regional process for workforce training, assessment, and certification, leading to the award of the Caribbean Vocational Qualification. The CVQ aims at facilitating the movement of skilled certified workers within the CSME, enhancing the quality profile and investment attractiveness of the work/labour force of CARICOM states and harmonizing TVET systems across the region. The RQF defines the different levels of the occupational standards.

There are five established levels of the RQF. These are outlined below:

- Level 1—semi-skilled worker/assistant (for example, a tradesman assistant);

- Level 2—skilled independent worker (for example, a mason);

- Level 3—supervisor/technical worker (for example, a construction supervisor);

- Level 4—manager, skilled professional, typically degree level (for example, a civil engineer);

- Level 5—executive professional, typically advanced-degree level (for example, a registered or chartered engineer).

4.3.3. Market Research of the TVET Syllabuses Examined by the Caribbean Examinations Council

The achievement of currency and relevance of the council's technical offerings and certification resides in the provision of school leavers with skills and knowledge required for them to make a meaningful contribution to the social and economic development of the region. In the face of these realities and consistent with its new strategic thrust in defining new directions in TVET, the council has conducted a series of market research between the period of 2009 and 2010 to guide the revision of all its technical and vocational offerings.

The major recommendations proposed in the market research conducted in 2009 for the CSEC industrial technology syllabuses are thus:

1. That the CSEC industrial technology syllabuses be revised with a view to incorporate higher cognitive, psychomotor, and affective contents, skills, and assessments required for entry-level job and lifelong learning.

2. That the council leads a continuous process of TVET guidance to the ministries of education, school leaders, administrators, teaching staff, and students. This is vital to dispel the poor image of TVET, to expound its potential and opportunities for development and prosperity of societies, to create enabling environments, and to get students of all abilities to be involved.

3. That the council leads the development of a demand-driven, flexible, integrated, and high-quality technical and vocational education and training system relevant to all sectors of the economy, including all levels and types of TVET. That it leads the process of stakeholders' involvement in all aspects of planning and policy making.

4. That the council leads the quality control leadership and monitoring roles of the secondary school system to ensure retooling, infrastructure, personnel planning and management, the best pedagogical practices, assessments, and resources to realise the achievement of the learning outcomes in the syllabuses. The council must exercise a proactive role in institutional capacity building (personnel, infrastructure, tools, and equipment) and use it to direct continuous improvement in delivery, examination, students' performance, and the socio-economic development of the region.

5. That the council facilitates the reshaping of TVET in the secondary education system through a regional re-engineering and marketing plan in the ministries of education (permanent secretaries, chief education officers, board members, and principals) and CANTA to garner support for an efficient allocation of financial resources, the imperatives for the operation and sustenance of a system of quality technical and vocational education and training based on the highest international standards.

6. That the council endorses and complements other developing and established national and international TVET programmes/systems through partnerships and quality assurance. The council must assess the scope of work of each entity, develop realistic budgets and manage them, explore mutual interests, manage differences, and support opening and integration into other developing programmes.

Given that secondary education is able to operate, administer, and certify TVET effectively (to get it right), then the transformation would have begun to address the right mix of labour and the right mix of labour force development for participation in the global knowledge- and technology-driven economy.

4.4. An Overview of Quality Assurance in Secondary-Education TVET

4.4.1. Definition of *Quality Assurance*

According to Shakes (2013), quality assurance is one component of a system of total quality management. It refers to administrative and procedural activities implemented in a quality system to ensure that the standard requirements and goals of an activity, product, or service are fulfilled. These are achieved through a series of systematic measurements, standard comparisons, periodic monitoring, and feedback loops that rely on evidence to confer performance weaknesses and assist in the development of plans to improve them.

4.4.2. *Current Strategies and Approaches*

Currently, CXC operates a moderated and quasicompliant system of quality assurance in the CSEC, CAPE, and CVQ assessment components.

i. Quality Assurance for CSEC and CAPE

Quality assurance relates to all the control instruments that are applied to safeguard the confidence, reliability, and validity standards of the marks and grades awarded in the school-based assessment component of the examinations. CXC employs the process of moderation as the main tool of quality assurance. Broomes (1997) describes *moderation* as a process of aligning the standards of different examinations or different components of an examination conducted in different places at different times and marked by different examiners. CXC's moderation process involves procedures prior to, during, and after the assessment of students. The requirements to fulfil each procedure are outlined in the syllabuses, mark schemes, and scoring rubrics. The school-based assessment is an integral part of candidates' assessment. It seeks to individualise a part of the programme to meet the needs of candidates, facilitate feedback to the candidates at various stages of the experience, and help build their self-confidence as they proceed with their studies. The majority of the SBAs comprise authentic assessments through projects or tasks. Students are required to apply knowledge to real-life situations, accompanied by reports or presentations.

Over the years, stakeholders' concerns regarding the SBAs continue to centre on the authenticity of the projects or tasks and the fairness that affect the validity and reliability of the scores that are awarded. Teachers' marks, however, may be adjusted as a result of the moderation process.

ii. Quality Assurance for the CVQ

With reference to the CXC TVET policy (2013), *quality assurance* is a systematic approach that uses a set of documented standards and evidences to verify the efficiency and credibility of the CVQ internal and external processes. The standards provide the assurance that the delivery and assessment processes are consistent and meet expectations with a high level of quality, reliability, efficiency, and environmental considerations. Quality assurance also acts as a monitoring process for institutions and provides information on their improvement status consequent to each audit. This ensures that institutions are managing and continually improving.

The quality assurance process employs three site audits that target and place a high premium on the evidence that shows the implementation of the roles and responsibilities of all stakeholders in the operations of the CVQ programmes. The evidences developed by the institutions in conjunction with the NTA / TVET council and ministries of education are aimed at achieving the performance criteria of the occupational standards and CXC's quality assurance criteria. It is important that the standards (occupational and facilities) and CXC's quality assurance criteria be used as guides in the development of these evidences. The requisite resources (physical plant, tools, equipment, materials) for delivery and assessment are guided by the facilities standards. These standards inform the facilities audits which are prerequisites for the commencement of the CVQ programmes. They are important tools that must be used annually to upgrade/improve the CVQ operations. Institutions, the NTA / TVET councils, and ministries of education are required to consult with and use consistently the occupational standards, facilities standards, facilities audits, and CXC's quality assurance audit findings and reports to improve and attain the internal and external quality standards for certification.

4.4.3. CVQ Quality Assurance Design

The quality assurance design consists of three main quality assurance audits and their respective instruments. The quality assurance audits are the following:

1. The prereadiness quality assurance audit.

2. The during-production/in-training audit.

3. The end-of-production/training audit.

The instruments consist of a set of criteria that makes decisions on the CVQ delivery, assessment, and certification standards. The administration of the instruments involves continuous checking/auditing in collaboration with stakeholders to validate standards, identify problems, suggest improvements, and train staff involved in the processes. Extensive on-site visits are conducted to provide information on the prereadiness audit, the during-production/in-training audit, and the end-of-production/training audit.

i. The Prereadiness Quality Assurance Audit

This audit provides information on the extent of the readiness of the institution to commence the CVQ. It is carried out before the commencement of the CVQ programmes to ensure the availability of adequate and quality resources and processes as outlined by the occupational standards and CXC's quality assurance criteria. The prereadiness audit targets the implementation of the roles of the NTA or TVET council, ministries of education, and institutions in the availability of the occupational and facilities standards, the completion of the facilities' audits, the completion of assessor's training by the teachers/facilitators, internal and external verifiers, and the availability of resources for commencement of the CVQ programmes. This is followed by an inspection of the institutions (internal and external) and completion of CXC's quality assurance instruments. A closing meeting is then held with stakeholders to discuss the findings and propose recommendations, which are documented in a final report. The report is submitted to the permanent secretary in the ministry of education in each participating country for corporate perusal and action.

ii. During-Production/ In-Training Quality Assurance Audit

This audit is not mandatory but can be requested by the institution to verify its operating standards at about 25 to 50 per cent completion of the CVQ programmes. The audit targets institutions' head and his/her management of the implementation of the recommendations consequent to the prereadiness audit. The implementation of the roles/responsibilities of partners in the CVQ organizational structure, incremental progress to achieving full compliance with the requirements of the facilities and occupational standards, use of the facilities audits, and the portfolio building and management processes for both teachers and students are also assessed. Weaknesses and problems are diagnosed, and action plans developed and implemented to address them. The action plan is a key evidence for evaluation in the end-of-production/training audit and should, therefore, be developed and implemented by the NTA / TVET council, ministries of education, and institutions. A closing meeting is then held with the stakeholders to discuss the findings and propose recommendations.

iii. End-of-Production/Training Quality Assurance Audit

This audit is carried out at the stage of completion of the CVQ programme, full or unit certification. Candidates would have already been registered for certification, with all the relevant internal reports and records of their achievement (internal verifier, the teacher, candidate and external verifier, NTA / TVET council, ministry of education, and the new portfolio building and completion status form and summary reports) completed, compiled, and organised for inspection. All recommendations from the prereadiness and during-production/in-training audits would have been implemented, and the institution would have achieved internally all the standards for the CVQ certification. The findings from the end-of-production/training audit are used in the certification process. The audits are done by a team of trained personnel who verify the extent to which the requirements of the CVQ occupational standards and CXC's quality assurance criteria are achieved.

4.4.4. Audit Procedures

Two types of procedures are proposed for administration of the audit instruments:

1. Self-administration of the quality assurance audit instrument.

2. Auditor's administration of the quality assurance instrument.

The instrument for the self-administration of the quality assurance audit is given to the head of institution and teacher/facilitator, who responds to the criteria, as read and explained by the auditor. This is followed by an audit sampling of the evidences and the areas that are rated 'compliant'.

The instrument for the auditor's administration of the quality assurance audit is completed by the head of institution and teacher/facilitator, who responds to each criterion, as posed by the auditor. The evidences for areas of compliance are requested by the auditor, followed by a sampling of the facilities and the exhibited evidences.

4.4.5. Institution's Compliance Rate

This quality assurance end-of-production/training audit states the compliance rate of an institution with CXC's quality assurance criteria. It is *not* a punitive instrument. It seeks to assist the institutions to progressively achieve *mastery* of the CVQ certification standards.

4.4.6. Report of the Quality Assurance Audit

A rubric is used to measure the compliance rate of the institution, as depicted in table 4.1.

Table 4.1. Compliance Rate of the Institution

Institution	Average of Head of Institution, Candidate, and Teachers/Facilitators' Audits Percentage
Head of Institution	
Teacher/facilitator	
Candidate	
Average	

Table 4.2. KEY for Compliance Rating

Percentage	Levels
100–85	Mastery
69–84	Proficient
53–68	Good
52–37	Developing
36–0	Developing

On completion of the quality assurance audit, a report of the findings and recommendations are generated and submitted to the CVQ stakeholders.

4.4.7. Award of the CVQ

The decisions for certification of the CVQ are made on the advice of the quality assurance findings and reports and the achievement of students reported in the following documents, which are submitted to the Examinations Development and Production Division:

1. External verification report.

2. Candidates' achievement sheet.

3. Facilities audit reports.

4. Candidates' portfolio completion form.

Whilst the quality assurance process for the CVQ appears to employ more transparency, rigor, and stakeholders' collaboration, limitations in the utilisation of the findings and recommendations continue to be observed. These can be improved by having more value placed on measuring institutions' TVET philosophies and policies; comprehensive stakeholders' involvement; graduate absorption, participation, and continuous upgrading in the labour market; monitoring; and evaluation.

4.5. Models of Quality Assurance System Operating in Selected Countries

Quality assurance is a component of a system of Quality Management. It refers to administrative and procedural activities implemented in a quality system so that requirements and goals for a product, service, or activity will be fulfilled. It is a systematic measurement, standard comparison, process monitoring, and feedback loops that rely on evidence to confer performance weaknesses and assist in the development of plans to improve them. An audit of the processes takes place to ensure compliance and to ascertain improvement.

Arising out of this review, three main models of quality assurance systems of varying contexts have been found. These models are as follows:

1. Compliance model.

2. Evaluative model.

3. International Organization for Standardization (ISO) model.

4.5.1 Models of Quality Assurance System Operating in Selected Countries

A periphery study on the context of operations of these models in the following selected countries is shared.

i. New Zealand

The evaluative and compliance models are used in New Zealand. The evaluative model operates in contexts that include self-assessment, periodic evaluation, and review. In the compliance model, the frameworks include institutional quality audit, inputs, and systems-based processes.

ii. Singapore

The compliance model is used in Singapore. The compliance model operates in contexts that include self-assessment, periodic evaluation, and review. In the compliance model, the framework includes a focus on outcomes, institutional quality audit, and continuous improvement.

iii. Australia

The compliance model is used in Australia. The compliance model operates in a framework that includes a programme-based regulatory quality assurance.

iv. The Philippines and Malaysia

These countries utilise the ISO model. The ISO model operates within a context of international benchmarking and continuous improvement.

4.6. The Demand-Led Quality Assurance

A typical demand-led quality assurance system aims at transforming the education and training system so that it offers the highest quality and value and equip beneficiaries with the mix of competencies to maximise economic growth, productivity, social justice, personal fulfilment, and lifelong learning. The skill needs of individuals, the economy, and the society are provided by a total quality management system that is planned and managed in a partnership involving institutions, government, stakeholders, and social partners. The involvement of industries, firms, and businesses is the driving force of a demand-led quality assurance system. Industry constitutes the following two main quality measures:

1. An input measure. Industry is involved in the development of the competency standards, curricula, and the assessments of the learners.

2. An output measure. Industry is involved in determining and implementing graduate endpoints, absorption, and continuous training in industries.

The demand-led quality assurance is rooted in the concepts of total quality management (TQM) and conformance to specification.

4.6.1. Total Quality Management

TQM refers to the management methods used to enhance quality and productivity in a business environment. It views the objectives of quality assurance as being specifically designed to constantly challenge an organisation's current practices and performance with a view to improve its inputs and outputs. Change management offers an avenue to align the mission, culture, and working practices of an organisation in pursuit of continued quality improvement. TQM works horizontally across the entire organisation. It involves all departments, all employees and extends backwards and forwards to include both suppliers and clients/customers.

Nel (2007) purports that a critical element of TQM method is that it is highly people-oriented and participative. It assumes that a quality culture is an integral and necessary part of an organisation. Each component functions as a quality interface. This approach assumes that all members of an organisation are responsible for quality assurance (maintenance and improvement). Quality is, therefore, not a centralised activity but devolves to various functions and organisational levels. TQM embodies five critical elements:

- The creation of an appropriate climate within an organisation for the establishment of a quality culture and empowering all members to take responsibility for quality improvement. An aspect of this climate is the creation of a dissatisfied state, a state in which critical questions are constantly asked about current inputs, processes, performance, and outcomes. This requires a process of research, analysis, and measurement of feedback aimed at improving the current state of operations.

- A customer-oriented maxim whereby customer requirements are agreed upon and customers are an integral part of the delivery. In TQM, the customer is both an internal and external stakeholder.

- Management by research, data, and facts. This principle stresses the importance of objective information from which an organisation can generate an assessment as opposed to subjective evidence.

- Has a people-based and participative management philosophy that stresses problem solving and seeks improvement opportunities in teams.

- Continuous quality improvement is the ongoing objective of TQM. It stresses that an organisation must remain cognizant of its purposes to strive for improvement. This sense of purpose guides an organisation in the allocation of its resources commensurate with its plans.

Quality within the TQM model is about systematic transformation. It deals with how criteria are shaped, how they are met, and who has the responsibility to meet them.

4.6.2. Conformance to Specifications

This concept consists of a set of clearly defined clauses or characteristics that describe a basic set of elements for developing and implementing a quality assurance system. The purpose of a conformance model is to control each step of a production or service to ensure that they match agreed technical specifications. Essential to this model is the documentary evidence that proves procedures have been followed and that quality has been achieved against predetermined criteria, specifications, or standards.

Some quality assurance systems that are used throughout the world and that are derivatives of total quality management and conformance to specifications are

1. the Malcolm Bridge NQ Award,

2. the European QA Management Award,

3. the Australian Quality Award,

4. the Koalaty Kid Program,

5. the Deming Prize,

6. the ISO 9000/2000 QM Code of Practice,

7. the South African Excellence Model,

8. the Balanced Business Scorecard, and

9. the Scottish Quality Management System.

4.7. Philosophical Postures and Bases of the Demand-Led Quality Assurance

Dewey (1916), in discussing the vocational aspects of education, believes that it should be an education that acknowledges the full intellectual and social meaning of a vocation. It will include instruction in the historic background of present conditions, training in science to give intelligence and initiative in dealing with material and agencies of production, and the study of economics, civics, and politics to bring the future worker into touch with the problems of the day and the various methods proposed for its improvement. In subsequent defence of his belief, Dewey advocates that the essence of vocational education should be the development of such intelligence, initiative, ingenuity, and capacity as shall make workers, as far as possible, masters of their own industrial fate. They must alter the existing industrial system and transform it.

TVET should aim for the development of individuals in all learning domains for meaningful living and gainful employment. This holistic development and the essence of TVET have been proposed since the twentieth century. The reality is that these TVET ideals are again relevant and have become the overriding philosophies of what TVET should be doing in the twenty-first century. TVET must deliver professionally successful graduates with the capacity of relating, responding, and adjusting to the intellectual and social facets of a productive, meaningful, and purposeful existence. Consequently, the following regional and international philosophical positions and bases have been selected to further the TVET reforms advocated for Caribbean secondary education.

4.7.1. Statement of the Ideal Caribbean Person 2000

The characteristics of this person include being diverse, respectful, emotionally intelligent, environmentally sensitive, democratically engaged, culturally grounded, historically conscious, entrepreneurially capable, and multiliterate. Such an individual is seen as someone who

- is imbued with a respect for human life since it is the foundation on which all the other desired values must rest;

- is emotionally secure with a high level of self-confidence and self-esteem;

- sees ethnic, religious, and other diversity as a source of potential strength and richness;

- is aware of the importance of living in harmony with the environment;

- has a strong appreciation of family and kinship values, community cohesion, and moral issues, including responsibility for and accountability to self and community;

- has an informed respect for cultural heritage;

- demonstrates multiple literacy, independence, and critical thinking;

- questions the beliefs and practices of the past and presents and brings this to bear on the innovative application of science and technology to problem solving;

- demonstrates a positive work ethic;

- values and displays the creative imagination in its various manifestations and nurtures its development in the economic and entrepreneurial spheres in all other areas of life;

- has developed the capacity to create and take advantage of opportunities to control, improve, maintain, and promote physical, mental, social, and spiritual well-being and to contribute to the health and welfare of the community and country; and

- nourishes in him/herself and in others the fullest development of each person's potential without gender stereotyping and embraces differences and similarities between females and males as a source of mutual strength.

4.7.2. UNESCO Pillars of Learning

The council has adopted UNESCO's five pillars of learning, which include the following:

- *Learning to know.* Learning to seek and acquire knowledge, values, and skills throughout life that are relevant to national development needs and priorities and responsive to regional and global issues;

- *Learning to be.* Development of one's personality, self-identity, self-knowledge, and self-fulfilment to be able to act with greater autonomy, judgement, and personal responsibility and family well-being;

- *Learning to live together.* Developing the disposition and ability to tolerate, respect, welcome, embrace, and celebrate difference and diversity and to participate and cooperate with others in increasingly pluralistic and multicultural societies;

- *Learning to do.* Acquiring the knowledge, values, and skills for active engagement in productive employment, community service, and recreation;

- *Learning to transform one's self and society.* Developing the ability and will to integrate sustainable lifestyles for self and others and to promote behaviours and practices that minimise our ecological footprint on the world around us.

4.7.3. Goleman's Emotional Intelligence

Goleman's emotional intelligence recognises that emotional health is fundamental to effective learning and breaks down emotional intelligence into the following five characteristics and abilities:

- Self-awareness—knowing your emotions, recognizing feelings as they occur, and discriminating between them;

- Mood management—handling feelings so that they are relevant to the current situation and reacting appropriately;

- Self-motivation—gathering up your feelings and directing yourself towards a goal despite self-doubt, inertia, and impulsiveness;

- Empathy—recognizing feelings in others and tuning into their verbal and non-verbal cues;

- Managing relationships—handling interpersonal interaction, conflict resolution, and negotiations.

4.7.4. Wagner's Seven Survival Skills for the New Economy, 2008

Wagner's seven survival skills are identified as those of the following:

- Critical thinking and problem solving;

- Collaboration across networks and leading by influence;

- Agility and adaptability;

- Initiative and entrepreneurship;

- Effective oral and written communication;

- Accessing and analyzing information;

- Curiosity and imagination.

4.7.5. Pragmatism

Pragmatism combines theory with practice. Theory is taken from practice and then applied back to practice. This is oftentimes referred to as intelligent practice. The educator and learner are both important to the learning process. Reality or real-world situations are stressed, context and experience are important, and the educator is progressive and open to new ideas. According to Miller and Gregson (1999), pragmatism (Reconstructionist strand) is the most effective philosophy for TVET since it allows new ideas to be considered for practice and it balances the philosophies between essentialism and existentialism. They have stated that vocational educators have been successful in terms of practice and keeping current and relevant through the use of the principles of pragmatism as a frame of reference and as a basis for workplace education. In linking skills training and the world of work, pragmatism has been responsible for the development of innovative programmes involving technology that allows TVET to meet the needs of the workplace of the future. Miller and Gregson have opined that the purpose of TVET is to transform work into democratic learning organisations. Existing workplace practices should be proactive rather than perpetuating. TVET should adopt a stand against injustice and inequity in work issues.

4.7.6. Progressivism

Progressivism is a component of the reconstructivism philosophical principle. According to Dewey (1938), the goal of education is to help student think rationally using student-centred approaches, project, and problem-based learning. Emphases are placed on experiential learning and the integrated curriculum that focuses on thematic units, integration of entrepreneurship in education, collaborative learning projects, lifelong learning, and social skills. Assessment is done by evaluation of learners' projects and productions and the integration of community service and service learning projects into the daily curriculum.

4.8. Features of the Demand-Led Quality Assurance

The demand-led quality assurance

- incorporates an underpinning philosophical principle that provides intellectual guidance and coherence to the quality assurance processes;

- instils a culture of quality and accountability from all levels of the TVET system;

- ensures that a TVET system has a strong capacity to demonstrate industry skill needs and standards;

- provides the means by which achievements are monitored, inefficiencies are detected and improved, and continuous progress is measured;

- ensures consistency of TVET outputs and helps raise the value of the TVET system; and

- provides assurance and objective evidences to management and stakeholders that an adequate level of quality is being achieved.

4.8.1. Principles of the Demand-Led Quality Assurance

- Quality is defined by customer requirements;

- Top management has direct responsibility for quality improvement;

- Increased quality comes from systematic analysis and improvement of work processes;

- Quality improvement is a continuous effort and is conducted throughout the organisation;

- The institution operates as a business in a culture of quality that focuses on continuous improvement and the delivery of high-quality products and services to stakeholders.

4.8.2. Imperatives for the Demand-Led Quality Assurance for TVET Programmes in the Twenty-First Century

TVET is a critical component of the achievement of Education for All (EFA) and the Millennium Development Goals (MDGs). As a result, UNESCO has placed increased emphases on TVET in the recognition of skills and their importance to educational development, labour market inclusion, and economic growth. In the Dakar World Education Forum 2000, TVET has been one of the four priorities of UNESCO Education for All strategy. TVET particularly contributes to EFA goals 3 and 6, as they relate to life skills.

Goal 3. For ensuring that the learning needs of all young people and adults are met through equitable access to appropriate learning and life skills programmes, improving all aspects of the quality of education.

Goal 6. Ensuring excellence of all so that recognised and measurable learning outcomes are achieved by all, especially in literacy, numeracy, and essential life skills.

The quintessence of the MDGs concentrates on human, social, economic, and environmental capital. A conscious and deliberate plan by all stakeholders to identify the right TVET programmes, their quality delivery, assessment, certification, monitoring, and evaluation is a prerequisite for the achievement of EFA, MD, and sustainable development goals. TVET programmes must be identified, delivered, assessed, certified, and quality assured for

- the many and varied needs of human development; and

- the inclusive societies (the people level).

4.9. Definition of a Conceptual Framework

As regards the study, a *conceptual framework* is a tool that provides a broad structure of predetermined standards and their indicators for guiding the accomplishment of an all-inclusive, comprehensive, and consistent quality culture in the management of TVET in secondary education in the Caribbean. It provides a number of headings of all the potential areas for which quality outcomes will be determined, classified, and prioritised to ensure consistency of the outputs of all parts of the TVET system.

According to Stockmann (2006), best practice organisations are managed through a network of interdependent and linked systems, processes, and truth. Any quality assurance must have a quality management system that includes policies, procedures, and review mechanisms to ensure that the necessary degree of excellence in training is achieved. A quality management system mostly consists of an organisational structure and resources that are needed to practice good quality assurance.

4.10. The Conceptual Framework for the Demand-Led Quality Assurance

Quality Assurance begins with the establishment of the quality system. This entails three stages, as outlined in figure 4.1.

Stage 1: Develop the quality assurance components and indicators.

Stage 2: Conduct the evaluation.

Stage 3: Use the result of the evaluation.

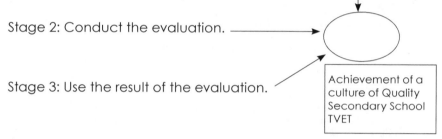

Achievement of a culture of Quality Secondary School TVET

Figure 4.1. Stages of a Quality Assurance System

4.10.1. Stage 1: Develop the Quality Assurance Components and Indicators

Quality assurance components and indicators must be based on established standards. Quality standards in TVET, according to Morris (2013), must involve all stakeholders in their developmental process. Achieving training and educational quality standard in the Caribbean should involve stakeholders, such as the TVET institutions, the local national training agency / TVET council, industry, the social partners, and the Caribbean Examinations Council.

The training and education quality standard defines the quality characteristics required for each institution. The standards are intended to improve the quality of the institution and are built into the institution's objectives. The standard is based on various educational components for which there are a series of indicators.

i. Functions of the Standards

- Helps to develop the quality of the institution and its products and measure its performance;

- Strengthens societal confidence in educational quality and institutional services;

- Facilitates decision-making on resource and financial allocations;

- Provides quality information to learners;

- Provides information to parents, industry, and government regarding institutional mechanisms and operations;

- Enhances transparency, equity, and accountability in training and education.

ii. Functions of the Indicators

- Assist in clarifying the educational achievements against set objectives as defined by the TVET standards;

- Outline the inputs, processes, and outputs of quality TVET management and which correspond to the duties and responsibilities of the institution;

- Contribute to the overall quality assurance achieved through self-assessment and external assessment;

- Encourage quality development;

- Benchmark international standards to support the development of quality TVET institutions.

4.10.2 Structure of the Demand-Led Quality Assurance Framework

The demand-led quality assurance framework comprises a series of core components and indicators that are designed to make judgements on the institution's quality practices. The core components provide broad indicators that can be monitored regularly. The indicators are descriptors or smaller elements that collectively contribute to the attainment of each core component. The structure makes provision for a comparative internal and external evaluation, as depicted in table 4.3.

Table 4.3. Components and Indicators of a Demand-Led Quality Assurance Model

Core Component	Indicators
1. TVET Philosophy	1. Total quality management principles and core values are developed, communicated to all stakeholders, and implemented.
	2. TVET policy, vision, and mission are developed, communicated to all stakeholders, and implemented.
	3. Strategic plan is developed and includes objectives that reflect the policies, roles, responsibilities, and capacities of the institution to develop competencies aligned with the socio-economic needs of the society.
	4. Customer- and market-focused activities are developed and implemented. TVET research and development are linked to regional and international labour market information systems (LMIS).

2. Human Resource Development	1. Sufficient and qualified staff is available to support each department of the institution (management, delivery, assessment, ancillary, industry relationships).
	2. An active staff-development plan is available and includes local, regional, and international industrial attachment and continuous staff professional development.
	3. Staff-management strategies are developed and implemented.
3. Physical Resources and Environment	1. Facilities standards are available for all programmes.
	2. Facilities audits are conducted, and the recommendations meet the requirements of specific sectors of the economy and for improving the quality of training.
	3. Occupational safety and health standards are developed and is operational for staff, learners, buildings, equipment, tools, and materials.
	4. Workshop ambience (floors, walls, roofs, windows, doors, tools, stores, equipment, safety lanes, protective clothing) adheres to OHS quality standards.
	8. Ambience of the general internal environment (offices, classrooms) adheres to OHS quality standards.
	9. External environment (buildings, grounds, water) adheres to OHS risk-management strategies.
4. Curriculum and Occupational Standards are Aligned to Industrial Standards	1. The approved regional occupational standards are utilised for the delivery and assessment of the programmes.
	2. An advisory system including stakeholders is in place to review curricula and advise on new skills requirements and training needs.

5. Training Delivery, Monitoring, and Evaluation	1. Programmes' delivery plans are developed, communicated to all stakeholders, and implemented.
	2. Establishment and implementation of a functional lesson-planning system with appropriate feedback systems.
	3. Internal verification personnel and quality reporting systems are established and are functional.
	4. External verification personnel and quality reporting systems are established and are functional.
	5. Systems for the use of results of the internal and verification systems are established and implemented.
	6. Teachers' and students' portfolio development and management standards are developed, implemented, and monitored.
6. Training Assessment, Monitoring, and Evaluation	1. Assessment plans are developed, communicated with stakeholders, and implemented.
	2. Internal verification personnel and quality reporting systems on assessment are established and are functional.
	3. Continuous assessment strategies to include individual, peer, group, research-based, and industry participation are established and utilised.
	4. Student record-management systems are developed and implemented.
7. Budgetary Allocation	1. A budget for the successful operation of each programme is prepared, approved, and received.
	2. Requisition and inventory processes are developed for regulating the use of the budgets.

8. Industry Linkages	1. Partnerships are developed with the industry and the social partners and are functional.
	2. The types of relationships encompass assistance with the delivery and assessment of programmes, work experience, and employment of opportunities for graduates, community service, and staff industry furlough.
9. Career Guidance and Counselling	1. An established system of career guidance and counselling system to provide career and vocational guidance and employment orientation to learners is in place.
10. Appeal Issues	1. Learners have access to an established appeal procedure that addresses issues in relation to the fairness and consistency of assessment.
11. Technology and Innovation	1. The delivery and assessment systems utilise information and communications technology.
	2. Innovative systems are developed utilizing ICT in the administrative, delivery, and assessment activities of the institutions.
	3. Partnerships are developed with local, regional, and international partners for the enhancement of technology and innovation.

4.10.3 Stage 2: Conduct the Evaluation

The process commences with an annual self-assessment of the institution, which is conducted by the local national training agency / TVET council and stakeholders.

i. Self-Assessment

Self-assessment is an important mechanism to improve institutional education quality. It involves quality evaluation by the institution itself in order to promote, develop, and improve quality and to be ready for the external assessment by the Caribbean Examinations Council. Self-assessment involves appointing a team leader and a committee to fulfil the assessment tasks. The end-of-production/

training strategies used by the Caribbean Examinations Council is proposed for this self-assessment.

ii. Objectives of the Self-Assessment

1. To audit and certify the present situation and evaluate the quality of the institution using defined indicators.

2. To motivate continuous self-development.

3. To connect each sector of the institution with their development plans.

4. The results of the self-assessment help the institution in its strategic planning, such as in

    *   staff allocation;

    *   budgeting;

    *   motivating the institution;

    *   helping to create confidence in the quality of the education offered by the institution; and

    *   encouraging a culture of quality and continuous improvement.

iii. Mechanism for Implementation

All institutions are expected to have a quality manager, assistant manager, and self-assessment team. These may be taken from staff, as defined below.

Staff: principal / vice principal / head of department, or experienced teachers/facilitators.

iv. Roles and Responsibilities of Staff

- Appoints the quality assurance manager / team leader, assistant leader, and self-assessment team;

- Provides policy and guidance for the implementation of the annual self-assessment;

- Provides the resources (staff, time, and budget) to assure effective self-assessment;

- Ensures the content and quality of the self-assessment report.

v. The Quality Personnel

The quality personnel manage the self-assessment. This includes

1. developing the assessment plan;

2. selecting and training of the assessment team;

3. supervising the conduct of the self-assessment of the institution; and

4. compiling and submitting the self-assessment report to the principal. This includes

   - the self-assessment report,

   - the assessment instrument, and

   - the list of the assessment team (quality personnel and team members).

A self-assessment report is generated and submitted to all stakeholders. The results of the report are used to improve areas of weakness.

vi. The External Assessment

Following the self-assessment, the examining body will conduct an external assessment of selected samples of institutions. The external assessment team consists mainly of representatives from the institution, the local national training agency / TVET council, and industry partners. A comparative assessment of the self-assessment report and the external assessment is done, and the findings are compiled and discussed in a postmeeting with the assessment team. The final rating of the institution is determined and compiled in a quality assurance audit report. This report outlines the major findings, the major recommendations, and the institution's compliance rate.

4.10.4. Stage 3: Use of the Result of the Evaluation

The quality assurance report is submitted to the Ministry of Education for distribution and use by stakeholders and the institutions. The report is not a punitive instrument. It seeks to assist the institutions to progressively achieve the quality standards for certification and development of the workforce for economic productivity and competitiveness.

4.11. Conclusion

According to Lok (n.d.), technical and vocational education and training (TVET) is the vehicle for the provision of education, training, assessment, and certification that is relevant to the needs and aspirations of the Caribbean Community. A proper TVET system speaks to a sound basic and secondary education as an important enabler within a seamless system of education and training. The role of the industry in defining the competencies within the internationally benchmarked occupation standards makes the TVET system relevant to the social and economic needs of the region.

As CARICOM strives to lead the process through the establishment of national training agencies / TVET councils, CANTA, and CXC, there is, inevitably, a greater urgency for stakeholders to play a more substantial role in the construct and operations of the learning infrastructure, experiences, validation systems, TVET outcomes, relevance, flexibility, access, and completion in secondary education. While the vision of CXC, an institution of CARICOM, is to ensure the global intellectual competitiveness of the Caribbean through the provision of quality assurance in education and comprehensive certification, an all-inclusive approach to the achievement of quality in radically reforming secondary education must be pursued by the council. The major readjustments must be embedded in the development of a mutual system for a shared understanding of quality assurance, the development and implementation of differentiated delivery, assessment, and placement approaches (on-the-job training, job shadowing, and apprenticeship) capable of meeting the needs of every learner and satisfying the foundational requirements for national, regional, and international labour markets.

This paper explores the benefits of a demand-led quality assurance and proposes a conceptual framework to stimulate discussion with a view to creating a culture of quality in the management of twenty-first-century TVET in Caribbean secondary schools. The ensuing benefits are the development of the region's human capacity required for workforce relevance, social and economic prosperity, and competitiveness beginning at the secondary education level.

It is the expectation that this conceptual framework will be ratified with further consultations with all TVET entities, professionals, practitioners, and stakeholders in the Caribbean. These are critical to the development of the inconclusive areas of the framework—for example, the development of the criteria and rating system and other tools desired for the effective use of the demand-led quality assurance framework. Additionally, it is the expectation that this chapter will contribute to the existing body of knowledge, principles, and procedures in quality assurance.

4.12. References

Barker, J. 2006. 'Address and Discussion: The Texas Association of School Administrators'.

Bernard, C. 2008. 'The CARICOM Single Market and Economy and Workforce Development and Certificate of Basic Labour Competencies'. A presentation.

Broomes, D. 1997. 'The Alternative Paper for School-Based Assessment'. Caribbean Examinations Council.

CAIC. 2006. Presentation at the Caribbean Forum for Lifelong Learning, Castries, St. Lucia.

Caribbean Examinations Council. 2013. Secondary Education, Draft Policy on TVET. CXC, Barbados.

Caribbean Examinations Council. 2008. Secondary Education, Annual Report. CXC, Barbados.

Caribbean Examinations Council. 2013. Secondary Education, Revised Draft of the CAPE Electrical and Electronic Technology Syllabus. CXC, Barbados.

Caribbean Examinations Council. 2013. Secondary Education, Revised Draft of the CAPE Food and Nutrition Syllabus. CXC, Barbados.

Caribbean Examinations Council. 2013. Secondary Education, Revised Draft of the Geometrical and Mechanical Engineering Drawing Syllabus. CXC, Barbados.

Caribbean Examinations Council. 2013. Secondary Education, Revised Draft of the CSEC Industrial Technology Syllabuses. CXC, Barbados.

Caribbean Examinations Council. 2013. Secondary Education, Revised Draft of the CSEC Home Economics Syllabus. CXC, Barbados.

Caribbean Examinations Council. 2013. Secondary Education, Revised Draft of the CSEC Technical Drawing Syllabus. CXC, Barbados.

CARICOM Heads of Government, Education Strategy. 2000. The CARICOM Ideal Person.

Dewey, J. 1916. *Democracy and Education*. New York: The Free Press.

Dewey, J. 1938. *Experience and Education*. New York: Macmillan Publication.

Goleman, D. 1995. *Emotional Intelligence*. New York: Bantam Books.

ILO Training Course. 2009. 'Promoting Effective Skills, Policies, and Systems: Skills for Improved Productivity, Employment Growth and Development'. International Training Centre, Turin.

Inter-Agency Working Group on TVET Indicators. 2012. Proposed Indicators for Assessing Technical and Vocational Education and Training.

Jules, D. 2009. 'Caribbean Examinations Council: Draft Policy on TVET'.

Jules, D. 2011. 'TVET: A CXC Perspective'. *The Caribbean Examiner 9* (1), a publication of the Caribbean Examination's Council.

Keating, J. 2007. 'Final Report: Matching Supply of and Demand for Skills: International Perspectives'. Published by NCVER.

Lauglo, J. 2006. 'Research for TVET Policy Development'. Published by InWEnt.

Lok, A. n.d. Concept paper for the development of a CARICOM Strategic Plan for Vocational Education and Training Services in CARICOM Single Market and Economy. UWI, St Augustine Campus, Trinidad and Tobago. consult@gsb.tt.

Mclean, R., and D. N. Wilson. 2009. *International Handbook of Education for the Changing World of Work: Bridging Academic and Vocational Learning.* New York: Springer Publications.

Miller, M., and J. Gregson. 1999. 'A Philosophic View for Seeing the Past of Vocational Education and Envisioning the Future of Workforce Education: Pragmatism Revisited'. *ERIC—Workforce Education: Issues for the New Century.*

Morris, H. A. 2013. 'Revisiting Quality Assurance for TVET in the Caribbean Curriculum'. University of the West Indies School of Education, St Augustine, Trinidad and Tobago, 21.

Nel, I. P. 2007. 'A Strategic Approach to Quality Assurance in Directed Education Training and Development, South Africa'.

Nyerere, J. 2009. 'Relationship between Technical and Vocational Acquired Skills'.

Stockmann Group. 2006. Best Practice Organization. Finland.

Shakes, E. 2013. 'Concept Paper for the Finalization of the Caribbean Secondary Education Certificate Syllabus in Industrial Technology'.

Shakes, E. 2009. 'CSEC Industrial Technology Market Research'.

Shakes, E. 2009. 'CAPE Electrical and Electronic Technology Market Research'.

Shakes, E. 2009. 'CAPE Food and Nutrition Market Research'.

Thompson, L. 2004. 'CXC and Certification in Technical and Vocational Area'.

UN Decade of Education for Sustainable Development. 2005. United Nation General Assembly, Resolution 57/254.

UNESCO/ILO. 2001. Revised Recommendations on TVET (R. 195).

UNESCO-UNEVOC. 2008. 'On the Way to Global Technical and Vocational Education and Training'.

UNESCO-UNEVOC. 2008. 'International Partnership Day on the Way to Global Technical and Vocational Education and Training'.

UNESCO. 1996. 'The Four Pillars of Education'. Report of the International Omission for the Twenty-First-Century Imperatives for Learning in the Twenty-First Century.

UWI/UNESCO. 2012. First International Conference on TVET in the Caribbean: The Montego Bay Declaration on TVET in the Caribbean on Technical Vocational Education and Training.

Wagner, T. 2008. 'Seven Survival Skills: 21st Century Schools'.

World Bank. 2007. 'Skills Challenges in the Caribbean: School and Work—Does the Eastern Caribbean Education System Adequately Prepare Youth for the Global Economy?' Report, Phase 1, No. 38555, Human Development Sector, Caribbean Country Management Unit, Latin America and the Caribbean Region.

CHAPTER 5

Review of Various Elements of Apprenticeship in Some Global Communities

Abdul Antoine

This chapter explores literature pertaining to apprenticeship and apprenticeship training. The literature appears from the Internet and is extracted from authentic sites/sources; these sites/sources are appropriately referenced in the document. Numerous articles have been written on various facets of apprenticeships. The articles predominantly focus on the merits of appropriateness to learning outcomes, workforce development, and benefits to persons—especially youths. Some common threads that are evident throughout the literature are that the apprentice (a) is required to understudy a person who is both skilled and experienced at what she/he does, (b) understudies such a person for a prescribed period of time, (c) receives both practical and theoretical information, and (d) receives a stipend. In most cases, especially in developed countries (USA, Australia, Canada, among others), a legislative framework that underpins apprenticeship activities exists, which ensures constant monitoring and improvement, when necessary, in keeping with market trends.

Apprenticeships are seen as the ultimate in cooperation between providers of career, technical and vocational education and training (CTVET) and the industry simply because they are based on a combination of work and study. In this chapter, it is assumed that all discussions on TVET encompasses career education. Apprenticeship systems that combine workplace-based as well as off-the-job training have proven to be successful in promoting learning and skill formation as well as facilitating employment by building bridges between the world of education and the world of work. Apprenticeship systems also facilitate the emergence and growth of new industries.

The ILO has noted that quality apprenticeships based on robust social dialogue and public–private partnerships have helped young people to overcome the work-inexperience trap that has blocked their transition from education to employment. Further, it has identified key success factors around which quality apprenticeship programmes have bridged training to productive and decent work (combining classroom and workplace training and sector-based approaches, incorporating entrepreneurship with technical training, combining training with earnings, providing access to social protection, and having respect for labour rights).

5.1. Introduction

Apprenticeships are seen as the ultimate in cooperation between CTVET providers and the industry simply because they are based on a combination of work and study (Smith and Kemmis 2013). Apprenticeships, they note, provide appropriate skills for companies and also all-round occupational and generic skills, including a tried and tested means of moving young people into the full-time labour market. Apprenticeship systems that combine workplace-based as well as off-the-job training have proven to be successful in promoting learning and skill formation as well as facilitating employment by building bridges between the world of education and the world of work. Apprenticeship systems also facilitate the emergence and growth of new industries based on technological and organisational innovations. Moreover, they are also seen as providing an opportunity to strengthen the skills required for a transition towards a low-carbon economy. Thus, they provide a source of skilled labour for an economy as a whole (IOE-BIAC 2013).

In this twenty-first-century economy, acquiring education, skills, and qualifications and continuing with lifelong learning is a necessity. To this end, the vocational training system offers one of the most practical means of acquiring and updating skills and ensures a source of qualified workers for businesses (IOE/BIAC 2013, 3). As postulated by Smith and Kemmis (2013, abstract), there are many different actual and potential models of apprenticeship that can be confusing for countries considering starting or redeveloping an apprenticeship system. Fuller and Unwin (2008) note that since medieval times, the term *apprenticeship* has been used to describe the journey a person takes from novice to expert in a specific occupational field. They have said that the concept transcends occupational boundaries and hierarchies and is used by surgeons as well as carpenters, chefs, actors, and musicians.

Apprenticeship is also the name for a set of formalised, state-regulated arrangements for vocational education and training (Fuller and Unwin 2008, 4). Gonon (2011) says that apprenticeship is a mode of learning, focusing on a specific learning site as well as a form of legitimate organisational setting in order to qualify and educate young adults for work and society. Enabling adults to receive full membership in an occupationally determined small community, apprenticeship historically used to be an informal arrangement of teaching and learning. Addressing the concept and general perspective of apprenticeship as they existed then, Gonon (2011) notes that 'apprenticeship was one (but by no means the only) type of TVET which suited the demands of trade and industry in a proper way' (p. 33).

This chapter is arranged in sections: etymology and definition of *apprenticeship*, apprenticeships as forms of work-based learning, the global appeal of apprenticeships, apprenticeships' inhibiting factors, apprenticeship framework, diverse apprenticeships, apprenticeship sponsorship and regulation, monitoring of apprenticeships, historical perspectives, and apprenticeships as effective policy tools. The document explores apprenticeship in Jamaica, the United States, Africa, Australia, Brazil, Canada, Germany, Norway, England and Wales, and Northern Ireland.

5.2. Etymology and Definition of Apprenticeship

The term *apprentice* is believed to have been around since the thirteenth century. The term morphed from Old French *aprentiz*, which meant 'someone learning'; the modern French term, *apprenti*, means 'unskilled, inexperienced'. The shortened form *prentice* has long been used in English since the 1300s (*Online Etymology Dictionary*, n.d.). Apprenticeship was well known in ancient civilisations, such as Ancient Egypt, Greece, and Rome, as well as in Asia; in Europe, the system of apprenticeship developed in the later Middle Ages (*New World Encyclopedia* 2012).

Apprenticeship is a system of training a new generation of skilled crafts practitioners. Most of the training is done on the job while working for an employer who helps the apprentices learn their trade. It involves a legal agreement as to the duration and conditions of the training. Often, some informal theoretical education is also involved (*New World Encyclopedia* 2012).

Christman (2012, 22) cites Brewer (2011) as indicating that many authors have defined *apprenticeship* as a form of education where a master craftsperson provides direct instruction to a student or an apprentice by passing on the skills and knowledge of the particular occupation. He also cites Keller (1948) and Miller (1993) as having indicated that in addition to Brewer's observation, apprentices were often taught how to act and conduct themselves in public and private.

Maryland's Department of Labor, Licensing and Regulation (DLLR) (2010) classifies apprenticeship as 'registered apprenticeship' and describes it as voluntary, industry-driven programmes sponsored by employers, employer associations, and jointly by management and labour. The Washington State Department of Labor and Industries (2012) refers to *apprenticeship* as a combination of on-the-job training (OJT) and related classroom instruction under the supervision of a journey-level craftsperson or trade professional in which workers learn the practical and theoretical aspects of a highly skilled occupation. After completing an apprenticeship programme, the workers' journey-level status provides an additional benefit of nationwide mobility at journey-level scale.

The International Labour Organization (ILO) is of this view:

> The expression apprenticeship means any system by which an employer undertakes by contract to employ a young person and to train him [or her] or have him [or her] trained systematically for a trade for a period the duration of which has been fixed in advance and in the course of which the apprentice is bound to work in the employer's service. (Apprenticeship Recommendation; R60, 1939, para.1) (ILO 2012)

The ILO notes that this definition incorporates some of the key features of apprenticeship, namely (a) is based in the workplace supervised by an employer; (b) is intended for young people; (c) fundamental aim is learning a trade / acquiring a skill; (d) training is systematic, that is, follows a predefined plan; and (e) is governed by a contract between apprentice and employer. The ILO's definition was reformulated in 1962 in its Vocational Training Recommendation (R. 117, 1962); several new characteristics of apprenticeship were identified. The definition that emerged read, 'Systematic long-term training for a recognised occupation taking place substantially within an undertaking or under an independent craftsman should be governed by a written contract of apprenticeship and be subject to established standards' (Para. X. 46). This later definition added new features to those previously identified (R60, 1939, Para.1), that is, (a) training to established standards for a recognised occupation and (b) long-term training.

The ILO notes that quality apprenticeships based on robust social dialogue and public-private partnerships help young people overcome the work-inexperience trap that blocks their transition from education to employment (ILO 2012). Further, the ILO identifies key success factors around which quality apprenticeship programmes bridge training to productive and decent work:

> Sector-based approaches sustain public-private partnerships and assure the quality of apprenticeship training and the quality of apprentices' employment; incorporating entrepreneurship with technical training inspires young people interested in starting their own business someday to choose apprenticeships and raises the social status of vocational training. Employment services expand young peoples' awareness of apprenticeships and the kinds of jobs they can lead to; work with smaller enterprises to

increase apprenticeship placements; and avoid gender stereotyping so that apprenticeships broaden career choices for young women and men; Combining training with earnings, access to social protection and respect for labour rights, apprenticeships open a first job for young people that can lead to career-long productive employment; and Combining classroom and workplace training enables employers to match training to their needs. (p. iii)

Of note, the 1962 ILO definition made no reference to young people, in contrast to the 1939 definition. The ILO (2012, p. 3) reported that a later definition again added more attributes to the definition. The organisation cites Ryan et al. (2010) as positing that *apprenticeship* has been taken to denote 'training programmes that combined vocational education with work-based learning for an intermediate occupational skill (i.e. more than routinised job training), and that were subject to externally imposed training standards, particularly for their workplace component' (p. 3). This definition, noted Ryan et al. (2010), recognised that, in addition to the attributes (seven) recognised above, regulated apprenticeship systems normally incorporated off-the-job education and training and external regulation of training standards both in and outside the workplace.

5.2.1. Informal Apprenticeship

Informal apprenticeship, according to the International Labour Organization (ILO 2012), is an important training system in many urban and rural informal economies. It notes that apprenticeship in the informal economy is a widespread phenomenon, including in G20 countries, and that in order to pass on skills from one generation to the next, poor societies have developed informal apprenticeship systems that are purely workplace-based. The organisation notes the following:

> A young apprentice learns by way of observation and imitation from an experienced master craftsperson, acquires the skills of the trade and is inducted into the culture and networks of the business. Apprenticeship agreements are mostly oral, yet they are embedded in the society's customs, norms and traditions. Countries in mediaeval Europe developed strong apprenticeship systems regulated by crafts associations, the guilds. Today, informal apprenticeship is an extensive training system in countries with large informal economies all over the world, including in South Asia, known as the *ustad-shagird* system. Variations in terms of practices are wide, yet the basic feature remains the same: the training agreement between a young learner and an experienced craftsperson to transmit the skills of a trade. (p. 4)

While formal apprenticeship is based on training policies and legislation, agreements for informal apprenticeship are embedded in local culture and traditions, with the incentives to participate on both sides rooted in the society's norms and customs (ILO 2011). Such rules govern aspects of the arrangement, including (1) how an apprenticeship is financed, (2) how long it lasts, (3) how the quality of training is assured, and (4) what happens if the contract is breached. These rules are enforced by social sanctions, reputation, or reciprocity. Under such arrangements, costs and benefits are shared. It notes thus:

> The costs for master craftspersons comprise the investment of time in training as well as, in many cases, allowances, in-kind remuneration (such

as meals) or wages; the costs for apprentices comprise their labour and often fees as well. Master craftspersons benefit from inexpensive labour and fees, while apprentices acquire marketable skills and an understanding of the world of work. (ILO 2011, 1)

5.3. Dual Apprenticeship: Linking Informal Apprenticeship with Formal Training Provision

Several countries, including Bangladesh, Benin, Burkina Faso, Mali, Niger, and Togo, piloted dual apprenticeship schemes in order to incorporate elements of theory, reflection, and modern technologies into informal apprenticeship. In these schemes, apprentices spent part of their training (15 to 40 per cent) in a 'training centre or vocational schools and master craftspersons receive skills upgrading courses' (ILO 2011, 5). Classroom-based instruction was delivered by training providers within the formal training system or by private or non-profit, non-formal training centres. Financing was commonly provided by national training funds, stemming from levies paid by large enterprises, or by international donors. To be most effective, a dual apprenticeship system needed to achieve the right match between the two sites of learning (the workshop and the training centre) in order that each part of the apprenticeship enriched the other to the maximum extent. Field trainers who visited workshops and business sites helped bridge the divide between the two.

Another challenge was the frequent lack of capacity in both formal and non-formal training centres to provide complementary training for large numbers of informal apprentices. To address this problem, in Benin, for example, the government provided incentives for the creation of new private training centres, many of them owned by individual master craftspeople Such incentives needed to be designed with care so they could be seen to be benefiting all the apprenticeship providers. Some dual systems introduced in the effort to upgrade informal apprenticeship could reach only higher-end segments of the informal economy—for example, if they required a certain level of education on the part of apprentices or financial contributions by businesses (ILO 2011).

The ILO (2011) realised the existence of a measurement challenge in relation to informal apprenticeship. The challenge concerned the lack of official records on informal apprentices, and it was thought that most countries where this system existed had only rough estimates of the number of apprentices in the informal economy. Statistical information about informal apprenticeship remained fragmented—therefore, if it existed—and some countries, it was noted, even included 'questions about apprenticeship in national household or labour force surveys', but very few distinguished between formal and informal apprenticeship (ILO 2011, 6).

5.4. Apprenticeships as Forms of Work-Based Learning

For many years, apprenticeship has been thought of as an outdated form of education. Visions of the early American colonist apprenticing under a blacksmith or shoemaker are a typical example. However, apprenticeships still exist and provide many advantages to individuals, schools, and businesses that make the bottom line investments (Stoner et al. 2011; Oates and Ladd 2011).

5.4.1. Work-Based Learning (WBL)

Work-based learning, according to Brown (2003), represents the integration of workplace experiences for students studying in technical education curriculum. It goes beyond the traditional cooperative education model to include a range of activities more aligned to vocational education and learning, such as apprenticeships, service learning, job shadowing, and internships. WBL, according to Harnish and Wilke-Schnaufer (1998), involves students in the building of underpinning knowledge by engaging them in real workplace tasks that create a context for creative decision-making in uncertain situations.

The European Training Foundation (ETF) (2013) posits that the term WBL cannot be clearly distinguished from other terms used to refer to practice-based learning in a work context. It notes that several close (and interchangeable) synonyms are found in literature, including 'employment-based learning, on-the-job training, enterprise-based learning and, in some contexts, workplace learning' (ETF 2013, 11). The foundation notes that the boundaries between these different forms of learning are often blurred, and the level of regulation and the extent to which they include a theoretical component varies. For example, Sweet (2011) is cited in ETF (2013) as saying the following:

> WBL refers to learning that occurs through undertaking real work, through the production of real goods and services, whether this work is paid or unpaid. It needs to be clearly distinguished from learning that takes place in enterprise-based training workshops and training classrooms. The latter is not work-based learning, but simply classroom-based learning that takes place in an enterprise rather than in an educational institution. (p. 12)

5.4.2. Workplace Learning

Research into literatures by various authors has unearthed an increasing awareness by stakeholders—that is, employers, employees, tertiary educators, and trainees—that workplace learning has become an important aspect of informal learning at the workplace. Previous studies indicate that learning at work is the most common way of learning for employees and, by far, exceeds learning in formal settings outside the workplace (Collin 2002). The Australian National Training Authority (ANTA) (2002) has defined *workplace learning* as learning or training undertaken in the workplace, usually on the job, including on-the-job training under normal operational conditions, and on-site training, which is conducted away from the work process (e.g. learning centre). The Australian Bureau of Statistics (NCVER 2003) defines *formal training* as 'all training activities which have a predetermined plan and format designed to develop employment related skills and competencies', whereas *informal training* is demarcated by 'training activities that are instigated by the individual or occur in an ad hoc fashion'. Harris, Simons, and Bone (NCVER 2003) argue that informal training is not merely an ad-hoc process but is part of a deliberate strategy that is inclusive of the work that requires action and the skills needed to do the work.

Skill New Zealand (2001) defines *workplace learning* as the formal acquisition of skills and knowledge in the workplace. Two possibilities of learning may occur at the workplace; firstly, the learning may be either 'employer-based', where the learner is an employee working and learning at their place of work, or secondly, it may be 'work-based', where someone who is not an employee of the company is there for the purpose of work experience or work-based learning. The formalisation of knowledge and skills in the workplace is obtained through assessment and the achievement of a national qualification. Workplace learning may be supported by additional education and training regularly or occasionally (Skill New Zealand 2001).

5.5. The Global Appeal of Apprenticeships

Apprenticeships are available all over the world in a variety of fields. Until very recently, in most civilisations, education is offered only to a small proportion of the population. Training, on the other hand, is provided in order for the large majority of the population who find themselves in employment of one kind or another to do their work (Winch 2013).

Christman (2012) opines that several authors have advocated for youth apprenticeship as a more grounded secondary and post-secondary pathway (Halpern 2009; Hamilton 1990; and Cantor 1997). Soares (2010) notes that post-secondary-level community colleges stand the best chance at impacting learning and workforce development. For example, the Apprentice School in Newport, USA, is highlighted as an exemplary model for the training it provides. This school provides a complementary blend of college-level academic courses and career theory (training).

The Organization for Economic Co-operation and Development (OECD) (2013) notes that apprenticeships are one of the longest-established arrangements for education and training where work placements play a significant part. Additionally, it notes the following:

> Apprenticeships are a core element of initial vocational education and training programmes (VET) in many countries and can combine on-the-job training with classroom-based learning in a variety of ways, ranging from apprentices attending school one or two days a week (e.g. in Austria, Belgium-Flanders, Germany, Switzerland), to alternating periods of several months on the job and in the classroom (e.g. in Ireland), to

school-based learning followed by workplace training (e.g. in Norway). Apprenticeships are found in the traditional trades and also increasingly in the service sector and in more highly skilled areas such as laboratory and hospital technicians. In Switzerland, for example, a new 'IT engineer' occupation was designated in the 1990s with an associated apprenticeship. (p. 1)

Jones (2011) opines that many other countries already have learned the lesson that, put simply, apprenticeship programmes can efficiently and effectively prepare students for jobs in a variety of fields. Jones notes thus:

In Germany and Switzerland, for example, apprenticeships are a critical part of the secondary education system, and most students complete an apprenticeship even if they plan to pursue postsecondary education in the future. It is not uncommon for German or Swiss postsecondary institutions to require students to complete an apprenticeship before enrolling in a tertiary education program. In this way, apprenticeships are an important part of the education continuum, including for engineers, nurses, teachers, finance workers, and myriad other professionals.

In the United States, however, apprenticeships generally have been considered to be labor programs for training students to work in the skilled trades or crafts. They are not viewed as education programs, so they have not become a conventional part of most secondary or postsecondary systems or programs. This leaves untapped a rich opportunity for the nation, as well as for the host of students who might find an apprenticeship to be an attractive route into the future. (para. 5)

5.6. Apprenticeships' Inhibiting Factors

The literature indicates that apprenticeship became less popular and almost disappeared after the Industrial Revolution. Barlow (1974) posited that increases in technology and efficiency in many occupations contributed to faster production and fewer needs for the master craftsperson, and thus apprenticeships became less viable. The Industrial Revolution led to major changes in the job market, and the lengthy time required for apprenticeships became unpopular for those wishing to enter the workforce and begin earning wages. For persons with academic interests and abilities, an apprenticeship was considered less attractive than receiving higher education at a college or university; thus, apprenticeships became unpopular. From an educational perspective, by the end of the nineteenth century, two negative movements further impacted apprenticeship and also prevailed in the United States, for example. The first was that of the practical arts movement, which stressed general education, including basic life skills; the second was that of the trade school movement, formally termed teaching a trade. As the debate grew over how much general education should be included with vocational education, it became clear that there was a general belief that workforce skills could be taught in a classroom setting, and apprenticeships, the idea of actually being employed in an occupation, became even less popular. There also seemed to have been inequity among individual apprentices in the apprenticeship systems. Winch (2013) cited Foreman-Peck (2004) as postulating the need for a 'sliding scale of remuneration'. Specifically, Foreman-Peck outlined the following:

There was a need for a sliding scale of remuneration that recognized the gradually increasing productivity of the apprentice, in order that financial responsibility could be distributed equitably between the individual learner and the employer. In non-apprenticeship systems this should be done through the taxation system. (p. 112)

5.7. Apprenticeship Framework

Smith and Kemmis (2013) have observed the following:

In Germany, responsibility is shared between the national government and the Federal States, while in France responsibilities are devolved to a local level. Systems can be hybrid: in the United States for example there is a federal Office of Apprenticeships, and 26 states have States Apprenticeship Agencies which assume some of the roles of the Office of Apprenticeship, while stakeholders in states without such agencies deal exclusively with the national Office. (p. 11)

The DLLR (2010) opines that apprenticeships are designed to meet the workforce needs of the sponsors. Because of a need for highly skilled workers, many sponsors use apprenticeship as a method to train employees in the knowledge necessary to become a skilled worker. This also means that the number of apprenticeships available is also dependent on the currency of the industry's training needs. Lerman, Eyster, and Chambers (2009) explained that ancient Egypt and Babylon organised training in craft skills to maintain an adequate number of craftsmen, and in the eighteenth century BC, the Code of Hammurabi required artisans to teach their crafts to future generations.

The DLLR (2010) notes that apprenticeships combine supervised, structured on-the-job training and related technical instruction to teach apprentices the skills necessary to succeed in a specific occupation. Such elements necessitate planning and monitoring in order to engender success. In England, for example, the traditional apprenticeship framework in the 1950s, 1960s, and 1970s was designed to allow young people (sixteen years old) an alternative path to GCE A-levels to achieve both an academic qualification at level 4 and 5 NVQ along with competency-based skills for knowledge work. The ILO/World Bank (2013) noted then that there were some 200 apprenticeship frameworks, with a further 118 listed as being developed in the country. Fuller and Unwin (2008) noted thus:

> The framework is useful to employers, as it allows them to think through how offering a good quality apprenticeship can contribute to their wider workforce and business development strategies. It is also useful to education and training providers to help them explore different ways to improve the learning opportunities available to apprentices both on and off-the-job. (p. 5)

The DLLR (2010) notes that there are 'apprenticeable occupations' and that a position must require at least 2,000 hours of training to be considered as one. The thinking is that if an occupation is 'apprenticeable', an apprenticeship programme will then be divided into on-the-job training and related instruction. On-the-job training has to consist of at least 2,000 hours per year of the apprenticeship, the equivalent of working full-time. On-the-job training for apprentices takes place at the work site under the direction of a highly skilled journeyperson. The related-instruction component consists of the classroom training apprentices receive to supplement the on-the-job training and teach fundamental principles of the trade. Each apprenticeship is required to have at least 144 hours of related instruction per year of the apprenticeship (DLLR 2010). In a study of eleven countries (Australia, Canada, Egypt, England, France, Germany, India, Indonesia, South Africa, Turkey, and the United State), data has been used to produce analysis to create a model apprenticeship framework. This framework consists of the following features: (a) a set of principles under nine major headings; (b) a listing of possible measures of success under four major headings (engagement, quality, outcomes, and public policy) and associated challenges; and (c) factors to be considered when expanding a country's apprenticeship system (Smith and Kemmis 2013). Apprenticeships are in-depth and certified, the minimum length of an apprenticeship being one year. However, most apprenticeship programmes take three to six years to complete, and successful completion of a registered apprenticeship leads to a nationally recognised certificate of completion of apprenticeship.

5.7.1. Diverse Apprenticeships

Although there are diverse apprenticeship systems operating around the globe, as may be expected, given differing national circumstances, widespread and common actions by employer organisations and/or companies include (a) advising governments on creating the framework conditions that make it less bureaucratic for companies to offer apprenticeships; (b) being involved in VET institutions and actively cooperating in setting up and designing the curricula; (c) raising awareness at company level about the benefits of apprenticeships; (d) advising companies when setting up apprenticeships; (e) supporting young people when choosing their career paths, for instance, through encouraging more and better collaboration between schools and companies; and (f) promoting the STEM subjects in school (IOE/BIAC 2012).

A wide range of programmes that can be broadly categorised as apprenticeship schemes exists around the world, from informal apprenticeships (which may be family-based) that are common in Africa and South Asia to the well-structured formal schemes of the so-called apprenticeship countries (Austria and Germany) (OECD 2012, 3). In Maryland (USA), for example, there are over 230 registered occupations and over nine thousand registered apprentices. Most apprenticeships are within the building trades and construction industries; however, there are also apprenticeship opportunities in nonconstruction occupations, such as child care development specialist. In sub-Saharan Africa, apprenticeships are reportedly available in a wide range of trades, mostly in blue-collar occupations, and are a substitute for school-based instructions (IOE/BIAC 2012). Gill, Fluitman, and Dar (2000) note that in South Africa, a new 'learnership scheme' has been adopted to broaden the existing apprenticeship system beyond traditional blue-collar trades to include white-collar occupations in the service sector as well as the informal sector. Haan (2006) reports that apprenticeships are less evident in Eastern and Southern Africa than in West and Central Africa, with the youth sometimes described in the former merely as helpers.

There are some programmes, according to the OECD (2014), that, while not formally referred to as apprenticeship schemes, offer young people a combination of training and work experience:

> Despite considerable heterogeneity across countries in the way apprenticeships programmes are set up and operate, these programmes tend to share a number of features, such as the direct involvement of the apprentice in the production process and the provision of some form of training by the employer. However, despite their potential benefits, there is considerable variation across countries in the scale of apprenticeship programmes. For example, over 15% of youth

aged 16-29 were apprentices in Germany in 2012, whereas apprenticeships are much less common in the Republic of Korea, Japan and the United States. In addition, in most countries, fewer young women than young men undertake apprenticeships. (p. 6)

5.7.2. Apprenticeship Sponsorship and Regulation

Apprenticeship is an internationally understood, long-standing, and robust model of learning and skill formation (Fuller and Unwin 2008). Apprenticeship is characterised by a contractual employment relationship in which a firm or sponsor promises to make available a broad and structured practical and theoretical training of an established length and/or scope in a recognised occupational skill category (Glover 1986). Registered apprenticeship programmes are operated by partnerships of employers, labour management organisations, and the government (IOE-BIAC 2012).

The ILO (2011) notes the following:

> 'Recommendation No. 195' suggests that government is primarily responsible for pre-employment training, while employers are responsible for further training and individual workers for making use of opportunities for education and training. One way of elaborating this key aspect of a national policy is to suggest specific policy actions, for example, mechanisms and incentives to secure the active engagement of social partners.
>
> They may include . . . strengthening of workplace learning, including apprenticeships or other forms of on-the-job training; public-private partnerships,

including joint management of training institutions and joint delivery of training, involving the public and private sectors and NGOs in improving outreach. (p. 3)

In the USA, many state economic and workforce development organisations developed strategies to facilitate collaboration between education and business for job training and economic development (Cantor 1990). For example, in Florida and Connecticut, the focus of preapprenticeship programmes was on the recruitment, training, and education of youth for gainful employment. These arrangements were designed to provide for coordination of a high school education, entry-level employment, and transition into post-secondary education. Additionally, these state economic development plans were configured to reflect national policy initiatives, such as Goals 2000, Tech Prep, and School-to-Work (Cantor 1997). Cantor noted that policy mandates were the primary reason why preapprenticeship programmes happened in some US states. Connecticut was singled out as having passed legislation specifically calling for preapprenticeship opportunities for youths. In Australia, the United Kingdom, and Germany, industry participation in the development, delivery, and funding of education and training is a major platform of education and training systems. All three countries have established arrangements to enable industry to have formal input into the development of competency standards and/or curriculum requirements that will guide the delivery and the assessment of vocational education and training (Misko 2006).

Conditions that exist in these countries do not permeate to other countries. In India, for example, it has been noticed that apprenticeship arrangements have remained underutilised due to the complexity and potential cost of reforming the system and the legislative base that underpins it (OECD/ILO 2011). Despite this, the following has been noted:

The Indian National Policy on Skill Development incorporates a range of initiatives that reflect international good practice, including the involvement of social partners in training delivery, for example through private-public partnerships, and in the certification process, along with sectoral approaches to skills development. (p. 3)

5.8. Apprenticeships as Effective Policy Tools

The OECD (2014) asserts that by equipping youth with the skills they need in the labour market, quality apprenticeships can be an effective way of improving employment opportunities for youth and promoting a smoother transition from school to formal-sector employment:

> In the first instance, they can provide a learning pathway for youth at risk of dropping out early from initial education. This is particularly important as the lack of a secondary qualification is strongly associated across countries with poor labour market performance. By combining work and study, apprenticeship programmes can help attract and retain youth who have become disaffected with classroom-based schooling and are better suited to learning on the job. (p. 5)

In addition, 'apprenticeships provide a good mix of basic competences and job-specific skills, they usually allow participants to earn a wage while studying, and they offer valuable work experience. These positive effects have revived interest in apprenticeship training' (p. 6).

In many countries, the OECD (2014) notes, until recently, governments have shifted their focus away from apprenticeship training to focus on raising university enrolment. This trend has since changed, with an increasing emphasis on strengthening vocational education and training (VET) and apprenticeship programmes in particular:

> Several countries have turned to the positive experience of Germany - a country with a long tradition of apprenticeship training - as an inspiration to revive existing apprenticeship systems or develop new ones. One such country is the Republic of Korea, which, in January 2014, began a dual system inspired by the German, British and Australian apprenticeship systems. Also, China is accelerating the development of a modern vocational education system that better integrates the worlds of education and work. (p. 6)

5.9. Monitoring of Apprenticeships

5.9.1. Jamaica

Jamaica's Ministry of Education (MoE) has joined forces with the Ministry of Industry, Investment and Commerce in reactivating the apprenticeship programme to provide skilled workers for the future logistics hub as well as the marine, business processing outsourcing, hospitality, and creative industries. A new Apprentice Board has been appointed by the MoE, following a prolonged period of inactivity. The new board has a mandate to initiate a review of the Apprenticeship Act of 1955 and to fast-track the provision of skilled workers through a revamped apprenticeship system. HEART Trust / National Training Agency has been designated as the implementing agency for the apprenticeship programme (HEART Trust / NTA 2013).

5.9.2. Germany

The National Vocational Training Act and the Landesschulgesetze (education acts at regional state or Lander level) set out the legal responsibilities of government, employers, and other partners, such as chambers of industry and commerce, education institutions, and trades unions, with regard to all aspects of apprenticeships. This social partnership approach means that problems and ideas are discussed between the key stakeholders to enable apprenticeship to evolve over time (Fuller and Unwin 2008).

5.9.3. United Kingdom

A key difference between the UK and many other European countries that have much larger numbers of young people in apprenticeships is that there aren't any statutory underpinning to apprenticeship in the UK (Fuller and Unwin 2008). The lack of a clear purpose for apprenticeship in England allows it to become a 'wrapper' or 'brand' embracing a range of formal and informal learning experiences, opportunities, and attainments, reflecting the diverse nature of around eighty occupational sectors (Fuller and Unwin 2008).

5.9.4. United States

Christman (2012) observes that the United States Department of Labor (USDOL) has provided oversight to apprenticeship programmes through its Office of Apprenticeship (OA). The USDOL (2004) has stated that the Office of Apprenticeship works in conjunction with independent State Apprenticeship Agencies (SAAs) to administer the registered apprenticeship programme nationally. Lerman et al. (2009) reports that apprenticeship programmes, referred to as registered apprenticeships, are owned and operated (sponsored) by employers or groups of employers, sometimes in partnership with labour unions. Registered apprenticeship programmes are operated by partnerships of employers, labour management organisations, and the government. Some twenty-nine thousand apprenticeship sponsors—employers, employer associations, and labour management organisations— have registered programmes with federal and state government agencies. Sponsors provide mentors, on-the-job learning opportunities, and required technical instruction to apprentices. Fuller and Unwin (2008) have noted also that perhaps surprisingly, given its generally laissez-faire approach to labour markets, apprenticeship in the United States has been underpinned by the 1937 National Apprenticeship Act, which provides a federal legislative framework specifying apprentices' contractual status and standards of provision, including their minimum number of training hours and their wages.

5.9.5. Australia

In Australia, apprenticeships (like all vocational training) have been historically the responsibility of state and territory governments; however, the Australian government has been playing an increasingly important role through the spending of (a) over $200 million per year for apprenticeship services to nongovernment service providers to provide a contact point for inquiries and to oversee the administration of apprenticeship contracts and (b) approximately $1 billion in incentives paid to employers, including commencement and completion incentives and extra payments for apprentices from disadvantaged or regional backgrounds. In addition, the government has provided tool subsidies to apprentices in eligible trades as well as new funding—from 2011—for mentoring and advisory services (IOE-BIAC 2013).

5.9.6. South Africa

In South Africa, the Business Unity South Africa (BUSA), government, and representatives of labour unions and youth formations have signed a Youth Employment Accord in 2013. The accord, which contains six broad commitments, represents commitments by constituencies aimed at promoting, supporting, and implementing youth employment initiatives (IOE-BIAC 2013). 'In support of the implementation of the Accord, BUSA is responsible for facilitating the development of the private sector implementation plan which contains company/industry/sector specific commitments and monitor progress' (p. 33). A number of companies implement various youth employment initiatives, such as (a) learnership (with an apprenticeship element in the delivery and execution in some programmes), internship, and apprenticeship programmes; (b) partnerships with further education and training institutes; and (c) youth development programme. There are twenty-one Sector Education Training Authorities (SETAs), which deal with a number of training initiatives, including placements (IOE-BIAC 2013).

5.9.7. India

In India, the Directorate General of Employment & Training (DGE&T) in the Ministry of Labour has the responsibility to implement the act in respect to trade apprentices in the central government undertakings and departments. DGE&T has six Regional Directorates of Apprenticeship Training for such a purpose, and state apprenticeship advisers are responsible for implementing the act in respect of trade apprentices in state government undertakings/departments and private establishments. Additionally, the Department of Higher Education in the Ministry of Human Resource Development (MHRD) is responsible for the implementation of the act in respect to graduate, technician, and technician (vocational) apprentices; this is done through four Boards of Apprenticeship Training. The main provisions of the act make it obligatory on the part of the employers—both in public and private sector establishments—to engage apprentices in 254 groups of industries covered under the act; make it mandatory to have five categories of apprentices (apprentices under the craftsman training scheme, trade apprentices, graduate apprentices, technician apprentices, and technician [vocational] apprentices) and to establish a Central Apprenticeship Council (CAC) to advise the government on the laying down of policies and the prescription of norms and standards in respect of Apprenticeship Training Scheme (ATS) (IOE-BIAC 2013).

5.9.8. New Zealand

The New Zealand government has recently announced a new approach to apprenticeship training after an examination of its current scheme has revealed that the system has not been working effectively and results have been disappointing. Planned changes to increase apprenticeship numbers—via a combination of all apprenticeships into a single nationwide scheme as well as a review of all industry training by the country's Tertiary Education Commission (TEC)—are ongoing. Planned changes are intended to increase apprenticeship numbers by combining all apprenticeships into a single nationwide scheme (IOE-BIAC 2013).

Effective 1 January 2014, the current modern apprenticeship scheme, together with other apprentice-type training, will be combined in an expanded scheme called New Zealand Apprenticeships. The educational content of apprenticeships is expected to be boosted, and Industry Training Organisations (ITOs) will have clearer roles and clearer performance expectations (IOE-BIAC 2013).

5.9.9. Norway

In Norway, both school and enterprises have equal responsibility for the upper secondary vocational education, and as the largest organisation for enterprises, the Confederation of Norwegian Enterprise (NHO) has a great interest in vocational training. As an important stakeholder, NHO actively contributes to the following committees: (a) the National Council for Vocational Education and Training, (b) the national council for each vocational education programme, and (c) the county vocational training board. The NHO has, together with the Norwegian Confederation of Trade Unions (LO), created an initiative to increase the number of businesses that contribute to vocational training. To meet these obligations, NHO has implemented initiatives, including (a) rallying government, together with the twenty-one sectorial member federations, to improve the school curricula; (b) approaching the government to facilitate more flexible training paths; (c) making sure that local schools and local business exploit the advantage of cooperation; (d) together with the Norwegian Confederation of Trade Unions (LO), creating an initiative to increase the number of businesses that contribute to vocational training; and (e) implementing a prize for members who are particularly involved in vocational training (IOE-BIAC 2013).

5.10. Historical Perspectives

Traditionally, vocational skills have been developed through apprenticeship structures. Secondary schools in medieval and Renaissance Europe focused on intellectual training in its narrow sense, educating an elite group of men in the liberal arts (Maclean and Pavlova 2013).

5.10.1. Jamaica

In 1834, the Emancipation Act was made into law by the British. This act allowed all slaves under the age of six to be immediately freed; other slaves served an apprenticeship for several years to learn helpful skills. Although emancipation was brought to Jamaica, the historic apprenticeship period came with its own problems since Jamaicans had to consider a form of cheap labour to guide them through the time it took for the emancipation of their former slaves to be completed. For example, although emancipation laws required former masters to provide apprentices with lodging and food, many owners charged for food or for rent in the form of extra labour. Another problem of apprenticeship was the division of labour hours. The apprentices were required to work 40.5 hours per week for the master, but the hours were not divided. While special magistrates fought for a nine-hour day, leaving the apprentices half a day on Friday as well as Saturday free for other work, planters almost always insisted on eight-hour days (Interactive Internet Websites Inc. 2013).

McLean (n.d.) noted that there were pending proposed changes to the apprenticeship act in Jamaica. Such changes would include (1) the flexibility to designate trades / trade areas / skills for apprenticeship training to focus on targeted areas (for example, Vision 2030), (2) the mechanisms for entering into agreements for training delivery, (3) the registration and monitoring of existing work-based training programmes under an apprenticeship scheme (example, SL-TOPS), and (4) the provision of recognised certification for skill levels achieved (McLean, n.d.).

The Heart Trust / NTA manages and organises on-the-job training through the School Leavers Training Opportunity Programme (SL-TOP) and the apprenticeship programme. The SL-TOP is said to be shorter and more focused on specific jobs or functions than ordinary apprenticeship. It is organised under a flexible framework and uses a skills development scheme that sets out the training content and minimum duration. On the other hand, the apprenticeship programme is required to use the board-approved trade order. Of note, men predominate in the apprenticeship programme, while women predominate in the SL-TOP programme. These programmes have not been NCTVET certificated; however, the technical framework is being submitted (Miller-Stennett, n.d.).

The traditional apprenticeship programme was formally transferred to the HEART Trust / NTA from the Ministry of Youth in 1994. It was structured with legal authority and trade orders that set the conditions of training. Apprenticeship training was regulated by the Apprenticeship Act of 1954, while the central organisation responsible for apprenticeship training was the Apprenticeship Board. The board's function was to establish and recommend standards of training for apprentices and facilitate the provision of skilled craftsmen to satisfy the manpower requirements of industry. In accordance with the legislation, apprenticeship contracts lasted from three to five years and made provision for a combination of institution-based and on-the-job training (Miller-Stennett, n.d.)

The HEART Trust / NTA provided training through ten institutes and academies, sixteen vocational training centres (VTCs), and on-the-job and community-based training programmes (Miller-Stennett, n.d.). The trust manages and organises on-the-job training through the School Leavers Training Opportunity Programme (SL-TOP) and an apprenticeship programme. Studies in the 1980s indicated reluctance on the part of employers to hire graduates of the programme who lacked working experience. Also, the apprenticeship scheme had progressively declined in recent times, with the number of persons enrolled and the number of contracts declining (Miller-Stennett, n.d.).

With a view to establishing a comprehensive national training system, the trust embarked on an extensive reform of vocational education provision and financing. Among the reforms pursued was reinforcement of the role of employers in the delivery of training. The trust also sought to move away from the traditional time-served apprenticeship system to a performance-based system within the framework of the new National Vocational Qualification (NVQ) of Jamaica (Miller-Stennett, n.d.).

The apprenticeship scheme experienced progressive decline, with the number of persons enrolled declining by 2.2 per cent to 1,353 in 1999. Also, the board was inactive, institution-based training was not enforced, and the number of contracts declined. The lack of tax incentive was partly blamed for employers' low interest in the programme; many employers preferred to employ youngsters under the SL-TOP programme, which offered a tax credit of $150 per week per trainee and imposed fewer duties and responsibilities on them (Miller-Stennett, n.d.).

5.10.2. United States of America

5.10.2.1. First Apprenticeship Legislation

The first legislation in the United States to promote an organised system of apprenticeship was enacted in Wisconsin in 1911. The law placed apprenticeship under the jurisdiction of an industrial commission. This followed the enactment of state legislation that required all apprentices to attend classroom instruction five hours per week. In the 1920s, national employer and labour organisations, educators, and government officials started a concerted effort to bring about a national uniform apprenticeship system. At the forefront of this movement were representative groups of the construction industry. The need for comprehensive training of apprentices had become a vital necessity in the boom days following World War I. Immigration was curtailed after the war, so fewer skilled workers entered from other countries. The combined effort of the various groups led (in 1934) to the participation of the federal government in the national promotion of apprenticeship. The Federal Committee on Apprenticeship, composed of representatives of government agencies, was appointed by the secretary of labour to serve as the national policy-recommending body on apprenticeship in the United States. It was to assume the responsibilities with respect to apprentices and their training under industrial codes formulated by the National Recovery Administration (Washington State Department of Labor and Industries [WSDLI] 2012). On the national level, President Obama (2009) referenced apprenticeship as an answer to the need to compete globally and urged all Americans to 'commit to at least one year or more of higher education or career training; this can be community college or a four-year school, vocational training or an apprenticeship' (p. 4).

5.10.2.2. The National Apprenticeship Act

This act (50 Stat. 663; 29 USC 50 states) was enacted 'to enable the Department of Labor to formulate and promote the furtherance of labor standards necessary to safeguard the welfare of apprentices and to cooperate with the States in the promotion of such standards'. Specifically, the act was formulated to (1) promote the furtherance of labour standards necessary to safeguard the welfare of apprentices, (2) extend the application of such standards by encouraging the inclusion thereof in contracts of apprenticeship, (3) bring together employers and labour for the formulation of programmes of apprenticeship to cooperate with state agencies engaged in the formulation and promotion of standards of apprenticeship, and (4) cooperate with the National Youth Administration and with the Office of Education of the Department of the Interior in accordance with section 6 of the act of 23 February 1917 (39 Stat. 932), as amended by Executive Order 6166, 10 June 1933, issued pursuant to an act of 30 June 1932 (47 Stat. 414), as amended (Sec. 2). The act gave the secretary of labour 'powers' to publish information relating to existed and proposed labour standards of apprenticeship and to appoint national advisory committees to serve without compensation (WSDLI 2012).

5.10.3. Africa

Traditional apprenticeships were seen as the most important source of skills training in Africa for the informal sector. These apprenticeships were noticeably concentrated in West and Central Africa (Haan 2006; Filipiak 2007). Approximately 70 per cent of urban informal sector workers in Africa were trained through this system (Liimatainen 2002). The Ghana Statistical Service, for example, reported that approximately 207,000 youths registered as apprentices in 2002. In this same period, a much smaller number, just over 50,000 youths, were enrolled by public and private providers (World Bank 2008). There were also related issues of access in Ghana, particularly for girls, in some areas of TVET (Palmer 2009). Evidence suggested that overall, most informal apprentices were males training in traditionally male trades (e.g. carpentry, auto mechanics, and welding), while young women had fewer opportunities in apprenticeship; those opportunities that did exist for women were usually in traditionally female trade areas, for which the market demand was often limited. The educational and gender fragmentation of informal apprenticeship training suggested that the poor, and especially poor women, were less able (either through cost, education level, or gender) to access the more dynamic and, potentially, more lucrative trade areas (UNESCO-UNEVOC 2013).

Traditional apprenticeships in the informal sector consisted of private contractual arrangements between a parent or apprentice and a master craftsperson who agrees to provide practical training in the workplace, ranging from several months to three or four years in duration, and subsequently certify the training in return for a fee or reduced earnings while learning (Haan and Serriere 2002). Haan and Serriere estimate that fees for traditional apprenticeships averaged about US$70 per year. The ILO in 2006 estimated fees to average US$160, ranging from US$22 to US$616. In 2005, Palmer (2007) estimated the average apprenticeship fee in the Ashanti Region of Ghana to be $42 with a range from $13 to $173.

Traditional apprenticeships in Ghana were distinguished from other formal apprenticeships that were registered with a government agency, usually a Ministry of Labour, and administered by employers and worker organisations. Traditional apprenticeships as individual contracts were self-financing and self-regulating and provided practical, hands-on training with good prospects for employment after the training. At the same time, traditional apprenticeships suffered from the weak education of those entering apprenticeships. Few passed beyond a lower secondary education, and many did not complete a primary education. Literacy was an issue. Choices of trades followed gender biases, and master craftspersons in turn did not provide theoretical knowledge alongside practical experience; outdated technologies were also taught frequently. Pedagogy varied, and there were few market standards available for judging the quality of the training provided (Johanson and Adams 2004).

In comparison to the formal system, Ghana's informal system originated as a means to reproducing skills within families or communities but were modified over the years to involve more formalised contracts, payments for training, and fewer restrictions regarding access to such training (Palmer 2007a). Informal apprenticeship training was said to be responsible for approximately 80 to 90 per cent of all basic skills training there, compared with 5 to 10 per cent from public training institutions and 10 to 15 per cent from nongovernment organisations and for-profit and non-profit providers (Atchoarena and Delluc 2001). Palmer (2009) noted that the general features of informal apprenticeship training in Ghana were said to be well known and similar to those described in other countries in West Africa. Johanson and Adams (2004) said that research done by Haan (2006), Johanson and Adams (2004), Palmer (2007a), and Valenchik (1995) were some examples.

In South Africa, the National Training Board (NTB), a tripartite policy advisory body to the minister of labour, was established in 1981. During the 1980s the focus of its work was on the apprenticeship system, and this work resulted in an amendment to the Manpower Training Act in 1990. The primary aims were at expanding the immediate narrow focus on apprenticeship training to incorporate a much wider range of training from unemployed youth programmes and entry-level training to the upgrading of skills and retraining (UNESCO 1996).

In Botswana, at the level of craft training, the apprenticeship scheme, which was modelled off the German dual system, was an important programme in terms of organisation and quality training. The training took four years and led to a national craft certificate. Approximately 75 per cent of the training was conducted on the job, a large proportion in private companies, and 25 per cent in government-funded vocational training centres (VTCs). Botswana's major concern was her inability to provide a strong industrial base than was available, since a potential trainee had to first find an employer who was prepared to sponsor the training before he/she could embark on the training (Adams 2008).

In Tanzania, many of the informal sector operators reportedly had a low level of basic and formal education, and training was mainly through direct apprenticeships within microenterprises. The 1994 Vocational Education and Training Act changed that situation by providing that the vocational education and training system should cater for the needs of both the formal as well as the informal sector of the economy, including training for skills needed for self-employment in the rural and urban areas (Adams 2008).

5.10.4. Australia

In Australia, the Vocational Education, Employment and Training Advisory Committee for competency-based training concluded in 1993 that 'there was an overwhelming consensus for an integrated approach to on- and off-the-job training' (p. 21). This viewpoint was subsequently reinforced by Hawke (1995, iii), who said that the 'effective integration of formal learning off-the-job with practice on-the-job provides the best of both worlds'. One investigation of integrated arrangements in Australia by the National Centre for Vocational Education Research (Mathers 1997) highlighted two key requirements for achieving integration: firstly, the need for one organisation to assume responsibility or take the lead in coordinating training, and secondly, the provision of a training framework supported by training and assessment resources that defined standards and served as a guide for training delivery and assessment.

The vast majority of vocational education and training (VET) students in Australia were said to be adults (covering the whole age range), and they studied part-time. Training was either institutionally based or workplace-based, and a sizeable proportion was through apprenticeships and traineeships, as part of a contract of training between an individual, his/her employer, and a training provider. Australian Apprenticeship Centres (AACs) provided training information to employers, apprentices, and trainees on rules and legislation as well as financial assistance that may be available. The centres provided support to employers, apprentices, and trainees throughout the traineeship/ apprenticeship (NSW Department of Education and Communities 2013).

Apprenticeship is said to be funded as part of the TVET sector in Australia. The TVET sector is funded jointly by the national and state and territory governments. Industry and private investment in training is also significant. Some of the funding provided through government was fully contestable and several Australian states introduced 'entitlement models', where the training dollar was tied to the student and they (or their employer) could make choices on the type of training and provider they wished to use. The Building Australia's Future Workforce package saw the establishment of the National Workforce Development Fund. This fund provided over $558 million over a four-year period to support training and workforce development, including the modernizing of apprenticeships (UNESCO-UNEVOC 2012).

5.10.5. Brazil

Brazil has a history of supporting apprenticeship schemes. Playfoot and Hall (2009) have said the following:

> [Fifteen to seventeen-year-olds] can join a two-year programme with employers on the Young Apprentice Scheme. This widely adopted initiative is considered to be highly successful. In fact, the rate of conversion from apprenticeships to full-time employment is estimated at around 70%. (p. 27)

UNESCO-UNEVOC (2013) has reported that young people of fourteen to twenty-four years of age who have concluded or are undertaking secondary / high school education can apply for apprenticeship scheme. These schemes are the following:

> Where they have a chance to get professional experience together with receiving a professional qualification offered by an educational institution that has established an agreement with the company. Apprentices are allowed to work not more than 6 hours per day. . . . The latter are offered by schools of the System S, technical schools or

officially registered NGOs. The maximum duration of the apprenticeship is 2 years as long as the apprentice is not older than 24. (p. 7)

5.10.6. Canada

Canada took a multifaceted approach to tackling skills shortages; hence, the promotion of apprenticeship training was crucial. There were apprenticeship training programmes for hundreds of trades in all provinces and territories. Jurisdictions actively promoted their apprenticeship programmes, especially to those groups traditionally underrepresented in the trades. Youth apprenticeship programmes existed in every province and territory to introduce opportunities in the skilled trades to young people (Matheusik 2012).

In Canada, the requirements to become an apprentice are clearly defined. Apprenticeship is a well-established form of work-based education that consists of on-the-job training and technical training. Apprenticeship is one of the main pathways to becoming a fully certified and legally licensed journeyperson in Canada. In some trades, a certificate of qualification may be granted to a trade qualifier or 'challenger' who demonstrates sufficient knowledge and experience in the trade to successfully write the provincial exam. While it varies according to trade, most jurisdictions require an individual to be a minimum of sixteen years of age and to have successfully completed grade 12 or an equivalent amount of related education and/or work experience to become a registered apprentice. Once these conditions are met, the prospective apprentice is required to find an employer sponsor to provide the on-the-job training. This employer must have a qualified journeyperson on staff to act as the apprentice's mentor. An agreement outlining the terms of the apprenticeship is signed by the apprentice and employer, and it is registered with and administered by the jurisdiction's apprenticeship authority or branch (Matheusik 2012).

Apprenticeship programmes typically range in length between two and five years, depending on the trade and the province or territory. Apprentices spend approximately 80 per cent of their time learning their trade in a workplace setting and the remaining 20 per cent completing the technical training requirements. Technical training occurs between four and twelve weeks each year and can be taken in a variety of formats, such as full-time block release or part-time evening or weekend courses. Technical training is based on industry input and may take place at a community college, an industry training centre, a private college, or even online (Matheusik 2012).

Upon completion of the technical and the on-the-job training components of the apprenticeship programme, the apprentice writes a provincial exam and, if successful, is granted a certificate of qualification, which is also known as a journeyperson's ticket. This provincial certification allows the journeyperson to work in the province in which the technical training has been completed and the skills and knowledge are assessed. Certified journeypersons are entitled to the wages and benefits established in their trade and are permitted to train and mentor apprentices.

To support mobility of tradespersons across Canada, a number of trades are designated as Interprovincial Red Seal Trades. Journeypersons who have obtained a Red Seal endorsement on their provincial certificate of qualification are permitted to work in any province or territory in which their trade is designated without having to rewrite qualifying exams. There are currently more than fifty trades included in the Red Seal programme, which accounts for close to 90 per cent of all apprentices and approximately 80 per cent of Canada's skilled trades' workforce. Work in a compulsory trade demands that an individual must have a certificate of qualification or be a registered apprentice receiving training in the trade. One does not need to be licensed, however, to work in a voluntary trade. The provinces and territories determine whether a trade is compulsory or voluntary (Matheusik 2012).

5.10.7. Germany

A dual system is established in Germany. Most youths pursue one of approximately 350 technical careers as defined by Germany's vocational education and training (VET) system. Training in the dual system combines theoretical education and on-the-job training. Trainees receive on-the-job training at companies as well as technical training at part-time vocational schools. Training is developed, implemented, and quality-assured by all relevant stakeholders, including the federal government, the Länder, trade unions, and employers' associations. The Federal Ministry of Education and Research (BMBF) is responsible for nonschool VET, that is, training that takes place in companies. All school-based VETs is the domain of the Länder governments, which are also responsible for all schools and education as far as qualifications can be acquired that are approved by the Länder governments (Ascui 2012).

In the dual system, the participating company and part-time vocational school share responsibility for training. The company signs a training contract with a young trainee and commits to passing on the required training outlined in the training plan. Training at the company typically occurs three or four days per week, which familiarises trainees with the technological and organisational aspects of the workplace. The experience allows trainees to contribute to the company's productivity, thus reducing the overall cost of training for the company and society as a whole. Trainees generally attend a vocational school for two days per week or in block teaching segments (480 lessons per year), where they learn the theoretical and practical knowledge of their trade. Students also take classes in modern languages or social studies (Ascui 2012).

Training occurs over a two- to three-and-a-half-year period, depending on the trade. In addition to training offered by companies, there are business association training centres where advanced training is available (Ascui 2012). The dual system is financed by private businesses that pay salaries to apprentices and by the state, which covers the budget of the vocational schools. In the early 2000s, there were approximately 484,000 companies (or 23.3 per cent of all companies) offering apprenticeships in Germany (Dybowski 2005). Germany's dual system results in a relatively low youth unemployment rate. It is generally lower than other European countries, at approximately 11 per cent in comparison to other European countries such as Italy (25.44 per cent) and Spain (37.85 per cent).

The combination of theory and practical learning in the dual system has created highly qualified professional artisans and specialised workers in Germany. Moreover, the dual system is often just the beginning of ongoing training for learners who go on to pursue additional education throughout the span of their careers. Although there are many positive aspects of the German system, it is not perfect. Some suggest that the information technology and communications (ITC) sector lacks a skilled workforce. Even allowing for these criticisms, however, global results indicate that the German system has achieved a high level of success over the years (Tremblay and LeBot 2009).

5.10.8. Norway

Vocational education and training (VET), including apprenticeship, was integrated as an equal part of upper secondary education and was regulated by the same acts that applied to general education. The Norwegian Directorate for Education and Training (NDET) (2010) reports that since 1976, Norway has had a unified upper secondary structure that coordinates general studies and vocational studies. The NDET (2010) notes the following about vocational education and training (VET):

> [It] is available all over the country so as to ensure an equal education for all and has since the mid 1990's, been organised in a '2+2 model', meaning two years in school followed by two years apprenticeship training in an enterprise. If it is impossible to provide enough training places, the county authorities are obliged to offer a third year in school leading up to the same final craft or journeyman's examination. In addition, specific groups are targeted, such as students with disabilities, adults, or pupils in remote areas. (p. 37)

Pupils could find an apprenticeship placement individually, or as in most cases, the county authorities helped with the provision. There was no individual right to an apprenticeship placement. However, if it was impossible to provide enough training places, the county authorities were obliged to offer a third year (Vg3) in school, leading up to the same final crafts or journeyman's examination. This was a costly alternative for the county authorities, and statistics showed that pupils who completed Vg3 in school achieved poorer results in their trade or journeyman's examination than apprentices. In 2012, there were about thirty-five thousand apprentices in upper secondary VET (NDET 2012).

By law, apprentices were employees of the enterprise and had the rights and duties as such. They were entitled to a salary agreed upon through a centralised system of collective bargaining. The salary corresponded to the amount of productive work the apprentice conducted. As productive work increased throughout the two-year apprenticeship period, the salary increased accordingly. The salary increased from 30 per cent to 80 per cent of a skilled worker's salary during the two years of apprenticeship. The apprentice was offered an apprenticeship contract, which was standardised and signed by the apprentice, the manager of the enterprise, the appointed training manager, and a representative of the county authority (NDET 2012).

5.10.9. England

Minns and Wallis (2012) posited that the formal structure of early modern apprenticeship was defined by rules established by guilds, cities, and the state. They noted that in England, the Statute of Artificers applied London's existing practices nationwide in 1563. While some details were negotiable, the core of English apprenticeship contracts was fixed by law, and apprentices served for at least seven years, working in exchange for instruction; the fruits of their labour belonged to their masters. Minns and Wallis noted also that although one recent survey of European apprenticeship concluded that 'the overwhelming majority of the apprentices did serve out their contract', existing evidence on how well apprentices fulfilled their contracts is ambiguous (Minns and Wallis 2012).

Results indicated that the rules and reality of apprenticeship in early modern England diverged substantially, and despite the law or guild and civic enforcement, the formal procedures of apprenticeship were frequently and consistently evaded. Many apprentices left their masters temporarily or permanently before their terms were completed (Minns and Wallis 2012). Misko (2006) noted that 'modern apprenticeships' enabled sixteen- to twenty-four-year-olds to undertake work-based training pathways leading to a National Vocational Qualification (NVQ) (Level 3) (in England, Wales, and Northern Ireland) or a Scottish Vocational Qualification (Level 3). They were initiated in 1995 in England and Wales and in 1994 in Scotland. There were more than 165,000 learners commencing a modern apprenticeship in England at the end of July 1999. By the end of July 2003, this figure had slightly decreased to 163,000 learners; the shorter duration, foundation apprenticeships, steadily increased across the time period, with advanced modern apprenticeships steadily declining. In 2003, the number of learners commencing a modern apprenticeship represented approximately 8 per cent of all sixteen- to nineteen-year-olds and approximately 4.5 per cent of sixteen- to twenty-four-year-olds (Misko 2006).

5.11. Conclusion

Modern apprenticeships can be seen as the ultimate in cooperation between TVET providers and industry as they are based on a combination of work and study. *Apprenticeship* is a system of preparing through training a new generation of skilled crafts practitioners. Most of the training is done on the job while working for an employer, who helps the apprentices learn their trade. It involves a legal agreement as to the duration and conditions of the training. Often, some informal theoretical education is also involved (*New World Encyclopedia* 2012).

Apprentices provide appropriate skills for companies and also all-rounded occupational and generic skills as well as provide a tried and tested means of moving young people into the full-time labour market. Although operating in the informal economy, apprenticeships are not unorganised: social rules and local traditions provide a conducive framework for training to take place. Upgrading redresses weaknesses in the system while maximizing its potential to benefit youth, small businesses, and more versatile and productive economies (ILO 2011).

It is of relevance to note that since time immemorial, people have been transferring skills from one generation to another in some form of apprenticeship. The records of Egypt, Greece, and Rome from earliest times reveal that skills were still passed on in this fashion. When youth in olden days achieved the status of craft workers, they became important members of the society. Apprenticeship systems—in keeping with modern tenets and workforce requirements—have gradually developed in the growing industries. Where it was previously focused at areas like the iron foundries and shipbuilding yards, it is presently seeking to embrace areas such as information and communications technology (ICT) and science, technology, engineering, and mathematics (STEM).

New generations of national apprenticeship programmes have emerged globally in the past three decades. They are governed by national qualifications frameworks (NQFs) and are strictly monitored for quality control purposes since they impact labour markets and workforce developments. They are regularly updated to take into account the changing skills needs of employers and are used by businesses to attract people from a wide talent pool into jobs and to train and retain them. Presently, a trend seems to be emerging that allows for the global movement of qualified and well-trained workers. One notes, for example, the free movement of Caribbean nationals among Caribbean countries and Europe's European Union with its single currency.

5.12. References

Adams, A. V. 2008. 'Skills Development in the Informal Sector of Sub-Saharan Africa'. World Bank.-

Ascui, J. 2012. 'Implementation of the Dual Vocational Education and Training Program in Chile, 1992–2007. *The Canadian Apprenticeship Journal* (7). Retrieved from: http://www.unevoc. unesco.org/e-forum/CAJ_7.pdf.

Atchoarena, D., and A. M. Delluc. 2001. 'Revisiting Technical and Vocational Education in Sub-Saharan Africa: An Update on Trends, Innovations, and Challenges, IIEP/Prg.DA/1, 320'. Paris: International Institute for Educational Planning. Retrieved from http://www.info.worldbank.org/etools/docs/library/251006/ day3skillsfortheinformalapril1se2.pdf.

Australian National Training Authority (ANTA). 2002. A glossary of VET terms. Viewed online at http://www.anta.gov.au, March 2009.

Barlow, M. L. 1974. *The Philosophy for Quality Vocational Education Programs*. Washington, DC: American Vocational Association.

Brewer, E. W. 2011. 'The History of Career and Technical Education'. In *Definitive Readings in the History, Philosophy, Theories and Practice of Career and Technical Education*, edited by V. C. Wang. Long Beach, CA: Zhejiang Press.

Brown, B. 2003. 'CTE and Work-Based Learning'. *ERIC Digest* no. ED482334. Viewed online at http://www.ericdigests.org/2005-1/ wbl.htm.

Cantor, J. A. 1997. *Cooperative Apprenticeships: A School-to-Work Handbook*. Pennsylvania: Technomic Publishing Company.

Cantor, J. A. 1997. 'Registered Pre-Apprenticeship: Successful Practices Linking School to Work'. *Journal of Industrial Teacher Education* 34 (3), 35–58. Retrieved from http://scholar.lib.vt.edu/ejournals/JITE/v34n3/Cantor.html#cantor.

Cantor, J. A. Summer 1990. 'Job Training and Economic Development Initiatives: A Study of Potentially Useful Companions. *Educational Evaluation and Policy Analysis* 12 (2): 121–138.

Christman, S. 2012. 'Preparing for Success through Apprenticeship'. *Technology and Engineering Teacher 72* (1). Retrieved from http://www.iteea.org/Publications/TTT/sept12.pdf.

Collin, K. 2002. 'Development Engineers' Conceptions of Learning at Work'. *Studies in Continuing Education* 24 (2): 133–152.

Department of Labour, Licensing, and Regulation (DLLR). 2010. 'Overview: Maryland Apprenticeship and Training Program'. Retrieved from http://www.dllr.state.md.us/labor/appr/approverview.shtml.

Dybowski, D. 2005. 'The Dual Vocational Education and Training System in Germany'. Keynote Speech for Dual Vocational Training International Conference 2005 in Taiwan, 25 April 2005 (slide 24). Retrieved from http://www.bibb.de/dokumente/pdf/a23_internationales_dybowski-taiwan_april-05.pdf.

European Training Foundation. 2013. 'Work-Based Learning: Benefits and Obstacles'. A Literature Review for Policy Makers and Social Partners in ETF Partner Countries. Retrieved from http://www.etf.europa.eu/webatt.nsf/0/576199725ED683BBC1257BE8005DCF99/$file/Work-based%20learning_Literature%20review.pdf.

Filipiak, E. 2007. 'Vocational Training in the Informal Sector: The Outcomes of a Field Survey in Seven African Countries'. A PowerPoint presentation prepared by the Research Department, Agence Francaise de Developement, Paris.

Foreman-Peck, J. 2004. 'Spontaneous Disorder? A Very Short History of British Vocational and Educational Training 1563–1973'. *Policy Futures in Education* 2 (1): 72–101.

Fuller, A., and L. Unwin. 2008. 'Towards Expansive Apprenticeships: A Commentary by the Teaching and Learning Research Programme'.

Fuller, A., and L. Unwin. 2008. 'Reconceptualising Apprenticeship: Exploring the Relationship between Work and Learning'. *Journal of Vocational Education and Training* 50 (2):153–171.

Gill, I., F. Fluitman, and A. Dar., eds. 2000. 'Vocational Education and Training Reform: Matching Skills to Markets and Budgets'. In *Skills Development in the Informal Sector of Sub-Saharan Africa*. Retrieved from http://siteresources.worldbank.org/INTLM/Resources/390041-1141141801867/2275364-1213970047519/Skills_for_Informal_Sector-6042008.pdf.

Gill, I., and A. Dar. 2000. 'Germany'. In 'Vocational Education and Training Reform: Matching Skills to Markets and Budgets'. Washington, DC: World Bank.

Glover, R. W. 1986. 'Apprenticeship Lessons from Abroad'. Columbus, Ohio: National Center for Research in Vocational Education.

Gonon, P. 2011. 'Apprenticeship as a Model for the International Architecture of TVET'. Retrieved from http://www.zora.uzh.

ch/50105/1/Gonon-Apprenticeship_as_a_model_for_the_
international_architecture_of_TVET.pdf.

Haan, H. C. 2006. 'Training for Work in the Informal Microenterprise Sector: Fresh Evidence from Sub-Sahara Africa'. UNESCO–UNEVOC (Amsterdam, Springer).

Haan, H. C., and N. Serrière. 2002. 'Training for Work in the Informal Sector: Fresh Evidence from West and Central Africa'. International Training Centre or the ILO, Turin.

Halpern, R. 2009. *The Means to Grow Up: Reinventing Apprenticeship as a Developmental Support in Adolescence.* New York: Routledge.

Harris, R., M. Simons, and J. Bone. 2006. *Mix or Match? New Apprentices' Learning Styles and Trainers' Preferences for Training in Workplaces.* NCVER, Adelaide.

Hamilton, S. H. 1990. *Apprenticeship for Adulthood.* New York: The Free Press.

Harnish, D., and J. Wilke-Schnaufer. 1998. 'Work-Based Learning in Occupational Education and Training'. *Journal of Technology Studies* 24 (2): 21–30. In 'CTE and Work-Based Learning' by B. Brown (pp. 1–5). ERIC Clearinghouse on Adult Career and Vocational Education. *ERIC Digest.*

Hawke, G. 1995. 'Work-Based Learning: Advice from the Literature'. Sydney: Educational Policy and Research Unit, NSW TAPE.

HEART Trust / National Training Agency. 2013. 'New Apprenticeship Board Targets Logistics Hub'. Retrieved from http://www.heart-nta.org/index.php/news-fix/220-new-apprenticeship-board-targets-logistics-hub.

ILO / World Bank. 2013. 'Towards a Model Apprenticeship Framework: A Comparative Analysis of National Apprenticeship Systems'. International Labour Organization, International Bank for Reconstruction and Development / The World Bank. Retrieved from http://apskills.ilo.org/resources/ towards-a-model-apprenticeship-framework-a-comparative-analysis-of-national-apprenticeship-systems/leadImage/ image_view_fullscreen.

ILO. 2012. 'Overview of Apprenticeship Systems and Issues'. ILO contribution to the G20 task force on employment, International Labour Office, Skills and Employability Department - Geneva: ILO, 2012. Retrieved from http://www.ilo. org/wcmsp5/groups/public/---ed_emp/---ifp_skills/documents/ genericdocument/wcms_190188.pdf.

ILO. 2011. 'Skills for Employment: Policy Brief'. Formulating a National Policy on Skills Development. Retrieved from https:// www.academia.edu/6900246/Policy_brief_Formulating_a_ national_policy_on_skills_development.

Interactive Internet Websites Inc. 2013. '1834–1838: Jamaica's History as a Slave Island Ends in Apprenticeship'. Retrieved from http://jamaica-guide.info/past.and.present/history/index.html.

IOE-BIAC. 2012. 'Scaling-Up Apprenticeships: A B20 Follow-Up Initiative'. Retrieved from: http://www.ioe-emp.org/fileadmin/ ioe_documents/publications/Other%20International%20 Organisations/G20/EN/_2013-06-18__IOE_BIAC_B20_Follow_ up_Initiative_-_Scaling_up_Apprenticeships.pdf.

Johanson, R., and A. V. Adams. 2004. 'Skills Development in Sub-Saharan Africa'. Regional and Sectoral Studies, World Bank, Washington, DC, Washington State Department of Labor and Industries (2007).

Jones, D. A. 2011. 'Apprenticeships Back to the Future'. *Issues in Science and Technology*, (Summer 2011). Adapted from a paper prepared for the 15 February 2011, American Enterprise Institute conference, Degrees of Difficulty: Can American Higher Education Regain Its Edge? (www.aei.org/event/100346). Retrieved from: http://issues.org/27-4/auer_jones/.

Keller, F. J. 1948. *Principles of Vocational Education*. Boston: D. C. Heath and Co.

Lerman, R., L. Eyster, and K. Chambers. 2009. 'The Benefits and Challenges of Registered Apprenticeship: The Sponsors' Perspective'. The Urban Institute Center on Labor, Human Services, and Population.

Liimatainen, M-R. 2002. 'Training and Skills Acquisition in the Informal Sector: A Literature Review'. ILO InFocus Programme on Skills, Knowledge and Employability, Informal Economy Series, Geneva.

Mathers, R. 1997. 'Integration of On- and Off-the-Job Training and Assessment'. Unpublished report, National Centre for Vocational Education Research.

Matheusik, D. 2012. 'Expanding Apprenticeship and Skilled Trades Opportunities in Canada'. *Canadian Apprenticeship Journal* (7).

Maclean, R., and M. Pavlova. 2013. *Vocationalization of Secondary and Higher Education: Pathways to the World of Work*. Chapter 2, e-publication, 346 pages. Published by UNESCO-UNEVOC International Centre for Technical and Vocational Education and Training ISBN 978-92-95071-57-5.

Retrieved from: http://www.unevoc.unesco.org/fileadmin/ up/2013_epub_revisiting_global_trends_in_tvet_chapter3.pdf.

McLean, G. n.d. 'Integration of TVET in the Formal Education System: The Case of Jamaica'. Retrieved from http://www. soeconferences.com/sites/default/files/PA3%20Integration%20 of%20TVET%20in%20the%20Formal%20Education%20System%20 -%20McLean.pdf.

Miller, T. M. 1993. 'The Historical Development of Vocation in the United States: Colonial America through the Morrill Legislation'. ERIC Document No. ED 360481.

Miller-Stennett, A. M. n.d. 'Informal Sector Training in Jamaica: An Assessment'. Retrieved from http://www.ilo.org/wcmsp5/ groups/public/---ed_emp/---ifp_skills/documents/publication/ wcms_103996.pdf.

Minns, C., and P. Wallis. 2012. 'Rules and Reality: Quantifying the Practice of Apprenticeship in Early Modern England'. *Economic History Review* 65 (2): 556–579. Retrieved from http:// onlinelibrary.wiley.com/doi/10.1111/j.1468-0289.2010.00591.x/ abstract.

Misko, J. 2006. 'Vocational Education and Training in Australia, the United Kingdom and Germany'. National Centre for Vocational Education Research. Published by NCVER ABN 87 007 967 311. Retrieved from http://files.eric.ed.gov/fulltext/ED495160.pdf.

National Centre for Vocational Education Research. 2003. 'Fostering Generic Skills in VET Programs and Workplaces: At a Glance'. NCVER, Adelaide.

NSW Department of Education and Communities. 2013. 'A Guide to Apprenticeships and Traineeships in New South

Wales'. Published by State Training Services. Retrieved from http://www.training.nsw.gov.au/forms_documents/ apprenticeships_traineeships/fullguide.pdf.

New World Encyclopedia. 2012. Retrieved from http://www. newworldencyclopedia.org/entry/Apprenticeship

Norwegian Directorate for Education and Training. 2012. 'VET in Europe—Country Report: Norway 2012'. Retrieved from http:// www.udir.no/Upload/Fagopplaring/internasjonalt%20arbeid/ UDIR_VET_report2012.pdf?epslanguage=no.

Norwegian Directorate for Education and Training. 2010. 'VET in Europe—Country Report: Norway 2010'. Retrieved from http:// www.udir.no/Upload/Rapporter/2010/5/VET_report_2010. pdf?epslanguage=no.

Oates, J., and J. Ladd. 2011. '50,000 Reasons Why Registered Apprenticeship Works'. *Techniques* 86 (3): 27–31.

Obama, B. 2009. 'Remarks of President Barack Obama: Address to Joint Session of Congress'. Retrieved from http://www. whitehouse.gov/the_press_office/remarks- of-president-barack-obama-address-to-joint-session-of-con- gress/.

OECD. 2014. G20-OECD-EC conference on quality apprenticeships for giving youth a better start in the labour market. OECD Conference Centre, Paris, 9 April 2014, background paper prepared by the OECD. Retrieved from: http://www. oecd.org/els/emp/G20-OECD-EC%20Apprenticeship%20 Conference_Issues%20Paper.pdf.

OECD. 2012. OECD note on 'quality apprenticeships' for the G20 task force on employment, 26 September 2012. Retrieved from http://www.oecd.org/els/emp/OECD%20Apprenticeship%20 Note%2026%20Sept.pdf.

OECD-ILO. 2011. 'The National Policy on Skill Development'. G20 Country Policy Briefs, India. G20 Meeting of Labour and Employment Ministers: 26–27 September 2011, Paris. Retrieved from http://www.oecd.org/els/48724080.pdf.

Online Etymology Dictionary. n.d. Retrieved from http://www. etymonline.com/index.php?search=apprentice&searchmode =nonehttp://www.etymonline.com/index.php?search=appren tice&searchmode=none.

Organization for Economic Co-operation & Development. 2013. 'Apprenticeships and Workplace Learning'. *OECD Skills Strategy, Spotlight No. 3*. Retrieved from http://skills.oecd.org/developskills/documents/ Apprenticeships_and_Workplace_Learning_SSS3.pdf.

Palmer, R. 2009. 'Formalising the Informal: Ghana's National Apprenticeship Programme'. *Journal of Vocational Education & Training* 61 (1): 67–83. http://dx.doi. org/10.1080/13636820902820048.

Palmer, R. 2007. 'Skills Development, the Enabling Environment and Informal Micro-Enterprise in Ghana'. PhD diss. (mimeo), Edinburgh: University of Edinburgh.

Playfoot, J., and R. Hall. 2009. 'Effective Education for Employment: A Global Perspective'. A report commissioned by Edexcel and prepared by White Loop. Retrieved from http://www.eee-edexcel.com/xstandard/docs/ effective_education_for_employment _web_version.pdf.

Ryan, P., K. Wagner, S. Teuber, and U. Backes-Gellner. 2010. 'Trainee Pay in Britain, Germany and Switzerland: Markets and Institutions'. SKOPE Research Paper 96, School of Social Sciences, Cardiff University. http://dx.doi.org/10.5167/uzh-48539.

Skill New Zealand. 2001. *Modern Apprenticeships News*. Wellington: Skill New Zealand Snell & Hart (2007).

Smith, E., and R. Kemmis. 2013. 'Good Practice Principles in Apprenticeship Systems: An International Study'. In: *TVET@ Asia* 1: 1–12. Retrieved from http://www.tvet-online.asia/issue1/smith_brennan-kemmis_tvet1.pdf.

_____. 2013. 'Towards a Model Apprenticeship Framework: A Comparative Analysis of National Apprenticeship Systems'. Retrieved from http://www.ilo.org/wcmsp5/groups/public/---asia/---ro-bangkok/---sro-new_delhi/documents/publication/wcms_234728.pdf.

Soares, L. 2010. 'The Power of the Education-Industry Partnership: Fostering Innovation in Collaboration between Community Colleges and Businesses'. Paper given at the 2011 White House Summit on Community College. Center for American Progress.

Stoner, G., B. Bird, and J. Gaal. 2011. '21st Century Apprenticeship: Embracing Nontraditional Partnerships and Technologies'. *Techniques* 86 (3): 27–31.

Sweet, R. 2011. 'Work-Based Learning in Vocational Education, with Particular Reference to Australia and Its Region: Models, Constraints, Opportunities and Benefits'. In European Training Foundation, prepared for an International Expert Panel Meeting on Work-Based Learning, Turin, 14–15 November 2011.

Norwegian Directorate for Education and Training with contributions from members of ReferNet Norway. 2012. 'Norway VET in Europe: Country Report 2012'. Retrieved from http://libserver.cedefop.europa.eu/vetelib/2012/2012_CR_NO.pdf.

Tremblay, D-G., and I. LeBot. 2009. 'The German Dual Apprenticeship System: Analysis of Its Evolution and Present Challenges'. Tele-Université UQAM, 2003. See pages 26–27 and 32: http://www.teluq.uquebec.ca/chaireecosavoir/pdf/NRC03-04A.pdf. 'From Dual System to Dual Labour Market'. Eichorst and Marx, IZA Discussion Papers, June 2009. See page 24: http://ftp.iza.org/dp4220.pdf.

UNESCO. 1996. 'The Financing and Management of Vocational Education and Training in Eastern and Southern Africa: Report of a Sub-Regional Workshop, Mauritius, 18–21 March 1996'. UNESCO: International Institute for Educational Planning (IIEP)/Industrial and Vocational Training Board (IVTB), Mauritius. Retrieved from: http://unesdoc.unesco.org/images/0010/001085/108538eo.pdf.

UNESCO-UNEVOC. 2013. 'Revisiting Global Trends in TVET: Reflections on Theory and Practice'. UNESCO-UNEVOC International Centre for Technical and Vocational Education and Training. ISBN 978-92-95071-57-5; e-publication, 2013, 346 pages. Retrieved from http://www.unevoc.unesco.org/go.php?q=Revisiting%20global%20trends%20in%20TVET%20Reflections%20on%20theory%20and%20practice.

_____. 2012. 'World TVET Database—Country Profiles: Australia'. National Centre for Vocational Education Research. Retrieved from http://www.unevoc.unesco.org/worldtvetdatabase1.php?ct=AUS.

USDOL. 2004. 'What Is Registered Apprenticeship?' Employment and Training Administration. Retrieved from: http://doleta.gov/OA/apprenticeship.cfm.

US Department of Labor. n.d. 'Registered Apprenticeship: A Solution to the Skills Shortage'. Retrieved from: www.doleta.gov/oa/pdf/fsfront.pdf

US Department of Labor, Employment and Training Administration (U.S. DOL, 1989). 1989. 'Apprenticeship 2000: Summary Report of Focus Papers'. Washington, DC.

Valenchik, A. 1995. 'Apprenticeship Contracts, Small Enterprises, and Credit Markets in Ghana'. *World Bank Economic Review* 9 (3): 451–75.

Washington State Dept. of Labor and Industries. 2012. 'History of Apprenticeship'. Retrieved from http://www.lni.wa.gov/TradesLicensing/Apprenticeship/About/History/.

Winch, C. 2013. 'The Attractiveness of TVET'. Chapter 3, e-publication, 346 pages. Published by UNESCO-UNEVOC International Centre for Technical and Vocational Education and Training ISBN 978-92-95071-57-5. Retrieved from: http://www.unevoc.unesco.org/fileadmin/up/2013_epub_revisiting_global_trends_in_tvet_chapter.pdf.

World Bank. 2008. 'Ghana: Job Creation and Skills Development Draft Report'. Vol. I, Main Document. Washington, DC.

CHAPTER 6

Changes in the Jamaican Tourism Industry and Their Implication for CTVET

Sheldon Thomas

Tourism has been part of the Jamaican history for many years and contributes to the economic development of the country by providing employment and foreign exchange earnings. However, crime, squatting, and distorted real economic benefits of the foreign exchange earnings are some of the factors affecting the industry. Career, technical vocational education and training (CTVET) is important to prepare the workforce to meet the demands of the tourism industry. This chapter seeks to review literature on the changes taking place in the Jamaican tourism industry and whether the current state of the TVET system can prepare the workforce to deal with such changes. Research has revealed that the current TVET system has been facing challenges such as poor performance in numeracy and literacy, financing, lack of single qualifications framework, and poor matching of training programmes with labour market needs. HEART Trust / NTA has been transforming its operations to provide quality training to the prospective and present workforce. However, it will not be able to train over 70 per cent of the workforce to be certified. This means that partnerships with other stakeholders will be important to address the deficiencies in the current TVET system to prepare a workforce that is able to meet the demands of the tourism industry.

6.1. Introduction

Tourism plays an important role in the development of a country's economy. Morris (2013) identifies tourism as one of the opportunities available for economic transformation and sustainable job creation in Jamaica and other Caribbean countries. According to the United Nations World Tourism Organization (UNWTO) (n.d.), *tourism* is defined as a social, cultural, and economic phenomenon that involves the movement of people to places outside their usual environment for personal or business/professional purposes. Tourism is seen as one of the growing economic sectors in the world and provides employment in sectors such as agriculture, construction, transportation, and small business. The tourism industry must respond to the needs of the visitors to remain competitive. However, there are economic, social, and environmental impacts of tourism in different countries. These impacts cannot be ignored as that can have a negative effect on the country.

It is important to look at how CTVET provides the workforce needed to meet the needs of the tourism industry in Jamaica. Tourism products are offered to attract tourists from different countries. Caribbean countries are losing their market share as they face competition from countries in Latin America, Asia, the Pacific, and the United States of America (Nelson 2012). Therefore, stakeholders in the tourism industry will have to make critical changes so as not to fall behind and become uncompetitive. One of the changes will include a dynamic and flexible demand-driven TVET system for the tourism industry to meet required standards, including customer service (PIOJ 2009). Training for tourism must not be restricted to hospitality but include other areas such as social and natural sciences and humanities to prepare for the changes occurring in the tourism industry (Boxhill 2004).

The purpose of this desk study is to review relevant literature that includes articles, studies, and statistics among others on the changes in the Jamaican tourism industry and their implications for the technical and vocational education training system.

In order to demonstrate that changes in the tourism industry have implications for the TVET system, two assumptions are made:

1. The Jamaican tourism industry continues to undergo changes in order to compete effectively with other countries.

2. Technical and vocational education and training systems in Jamaica have to be dynamic in order to provide a workforce that can meet the changes in the tourism industry.

The review is divided into four main parts:

1. Historical and current background to the Jamaican tourism industry

2. Importance of tourism to the Jamaican economy

3. Importance of technical and vocational education and training (TVET) system in addressing the changes in the tourism industry in Jamaica

4. Conclusion and recommendations to improve the TVET system to address the changes in the tourism industry

6.2. Historical and Current Background to the Jamaican Tourism Industry

According to the Jamaica Tourist Board (n.d.), 1890 was the beginning of Jamaican government's commitment to the development of the island's tourism sector when a Jamaican International Exhibition was planned for 1891 and the Jamaica Hotels Law was passed in 1890 to encourage hotel constructions to accommodate these visitors. Prior to 1890, the industry was disorganised. The infrastructure available was inadequate and needed appropriate servicing. The one-hundred-room Constant Spring Hotel, which was built in 1888, as well as a number of lodging houses and inns existed. The hotels built for the exhibition and within that period were Myrtle Bank, Queens, Hotel Rio Cobre, Moneague Hotel, Titchfield Hotel, and Mandeville Hotel. Jamaica sought assistance from the United States in managing and developing the local tourism workforce, especially in the area of methods to improve attitude towards the industry. There was a concern that Jamaica was depending too much on the United States; therefore, London implemented the Imperial Direct Line to develop a market for the banana trade independent of the United States. This venture was operated by Elder Dempster and Company, which also leased the Myrtle Bank and Constant Spring Hotels from government, and started to advertise them. This led to an increase in the number of visitors to the island.

According to Taylor (1993), attempts to organise a bureau responsible for marketing Jamaica resulted in the formation of the Jamaica Tourist Association in 1910. He further explained that the primary purpose of this association was to enhance Jamaica as a health and pleasure resort and give information to prospective visitors and those already on the island. The Jamaican government established the Tourist Trade Development Board in 1922. Problems began to surface about the financing of the new promotional entity as the promotion of the tourism product was seen as a private concern. In order to settle this matter, the government passed a law in 1935 to impose duty on passengers transported to Jamaica by a ship or aircraft in order to raise funds for advertising the Jamaican tourism product. This programme and political developments in the Caribbean and the world led to the growth of Jamaica's tourism in the 1930s.

The government recognised the need for a more effective organisation than the Tourist Trade Development Board, which led to the establishment of the Jamaica Tourist Board in 1955, with a membership that reflected all interests in the industry. It operated under the Ministry of Trade and Industry and was financed by annual grants and given special borrowing powers. Tourism in Jamaica was viewed as a tool for economic development as the country moved away from the agricultural economy due to decline in sugar exports. Persons felt that Jamaica had natural resources such as sand, sun, and sea and the friendliness of the people to attract visitors to the island.

The end of World War II ushered in the air age and the beginnings of mass international travel. The adoption of guaranteed holidays with pay for most North American and European workers allowed more people to travel (Gmelch 2012). Travel agencies and tour operators promoted the Caribbean as the exotic tropical place for winter vacations. The term *mass tourism* was coined as the Caribbean holiday package, which was within the price range of middle-income families. This led to the increase in the number of tourists to the Caribbean.

During the period between 1961 and 1963, the tourism industry declined and the newly independent government of Jamaica realised the need to revive and expand this sector. The Jamaica Hotel and Tourist Association was established in 1961 to tackle hotel problems and represent the interests of hoteliers to the tourist board and the Jamaican government. A director of tourism was appointed in 1963. These establishments started Jamaica's intensive promotional efforts to improve the tourism industry. The Jamaica Hotels Aids Law was amended in 1963 to provide importation on a duty-free basis on building materials, furniture, and equipment for new hotels or upgrade to existing ones (Taylor 1993). The Jamaica Association of Villas and Apartments was established in 1967 to provide representation for small properties (Jamaica Tourist Board, n.d.).

In the 1970s, Jamaica faced problems such as increased competition from neighbouring countries such as Bahamas and Barbados, rising fuel prices that affected airline costs, and political and social unrest in the island that led to negative press coverage overseas. When there was an increase in the cost of oil price, Jamaica developed strategies to appeal to Jamaicans to travel in their own country rather than abroad and Jamaicans living abroad to spend their holidays in Jamaica (Nelson 2012). These factors caused a fluctuation in the number of tourist arrivals to Jamaica. However, after the 1980 general election, there was an increase in tourist arrivals due to reduction in political unrest and renewed confidence in Jamaica's future and immense advertising by the Jamaica Tourist Board. By 1982, tourism became Jamaica's main source of foreign exchange as the bauxite industry profits declined (Rhiney 2012).

There was continuation of growth in tourist arrivals to Jamaica between 1990 and 2000, despite the impact of Hurricane Gilbert, the Persian Gulf War, and the US and Canadian economic recessions. Table 6.1 shows the total tourist arrivals from 1955 to 2012, showing an increase despite the number of setbacks affecting the industry.

Table 6.1. Total Visitors Arrivals and Expenditure in Jamaica

Year	Total Stopover Arrivals	Total Cruise Arrivals	Total Visitor Arrivals	Total Visitor Expenditure (Estimated)
1955	86,793	35,356	122,149	£6,718,190
1963	131,865	70,464	202,329	£13,500,000
1975	395,809	150,433	553,258	US$128,706,000
1984	603,436	231,039	843,774	US$406,600,000
1994	976,635	595,036	1,108,871	US$919,000,000
2003	1,350,285	1,132,596	2,482,881	US$1,336,000,000
2009	1,831,097	922,349	2,753,446	US$1,925,423,000
2010	1,921,678	909,619	2,831,297	US$2,001,244,000
2011	1,951,752	1,125,481	3,077,233	US$2,008,343,000
2012	1,986,085	1,320,083	3,306,168	US$2,069,568,000

Jamaica converted from the English pound to the Jamaican dollar in 1969

Adapted from Jamaica Tourist Board (n.d.). Tourism in Jamaica and Jamaica Tourist Board, 2012. *Annual travel statistics, p. 208.*

6.3. Global Trends in Tourism

According to the World Tourism Organization (UNWTO) (2012), international tourist arrivals (overnight visitors) worldwide surpassed 1 billion (1,035 billion) for the first time in history in 2012 despite continued economic instability around the globe. This was an additional 39 million international tourists up from 996 million in 2011. UNWTO is the United Nations agency responsible for the promotion of responsible, sustainable, and universally accessible tourism. This organisation predicted the following in a 2011 study to shape tourism's development over the next two decades:

- International tourist arrivals will reach close to 1.4 billion in 2020 and hit 1.8 billion by 2030.

- In 2030, five million people will be crossing international borders for leisure, business, or other purposes every day.

- In 2015, emerging economies will, for the first time in history, receive more international tourist arrivals than advanced ones, receiving one billion arrivals by 2030.

- Arrivals for visiting friends and family, health, religion, and other purposes will grow slightly faster than arrivals for leisure or business.

In 2012, 52 per cent or 536 million international tourists travelled for leisure, recreation, and holidays, 27 per cent of the tourists reported that they travelled for health treatment, visiting friends, and relatives and religion, 14 per cent of them travelled for business and professional reasons, and 7 per cent of arrivals were not specified (UNWTO 2013).

According to UNWTO (2012 and 2013), the growth in international tourism receipts matched the growth in arrivals. In 2012, the receipts grew by 4 per cent in real terms and reached a new record of US$1,075 billion worldwide (euro 837 billion). This corresponds to growth in international tourist arrivals, which also advanced by 4 per cent, and this confirms that there is a strong connection between both receipts and arrivals.

The top spenders in international tourism in 2012 were China, Germany, United States, United Kingdom, Russian Federation, France, Canada, Japan, Australia, and Italy (UNWTO 2013). Chinese tourism spending has been increased from US$13 billion in 2000 to US$102 billion due to rise in disposable incomes, a relaxation of restrictions on foreign travel, and an appreciating currency. China has overturned long-time top spender Germany (US$84 billion) and second largest spender United States (US$83 billion).

In the Americas, which include North America, Central, South America, and the Caribbean, the top ten destinations in 2012 were United States, Mexico, Canada, Brazil, Argentina, Dominican Republic, Chile, Puerto Rico, Peru, and Uruguay (UNWTO 2013). North America has the highest tourist arrivals with 106,683, followed by South America with 26,673; the Caribbean has 20,887, Central America with 8,872 tourist arrivals.

The long-term trends in global tourism include growth in youth travel market, ecotourism, holistic tourism, and importance of information and communication technologies (ICTs) and online travel services (Tourism Task Force 2009). There is a change in the consumer tastes and behaviour, and one of the demands is holistic treatment in terms of health and wellness. Customers have more choices and are becoming more selective in their choices based on their demands. The global trend is not in the direction of sea and sand tourism but in other areas, such as heritage, cultural attraction, and green tourism (Boxill 2004). Information technology will reshape the way we live, work, and play as the technology is used in the operations of the airline, hotel, and food and beverage industries (Charles 2002). Through the use of the Internet, tourism products are marketed and consumers are able to search for tourism destinations worldwide and make their reservations to travel online. According to Zappino (2005) and Tourism Taskforce (2009), the new type of tourists is increasingly aware about the importance of respecting the environment and interested in 'going green'. The new trendy words in international tourism and travel are *natural, green, eco-friendly,* and *sustainable*. The UN General Assembly in 2012 totally adopted a resolution stressing ecotourism's role in the fight against poverty and protection of the environment, and governments are called upon to promote investment in this type of tourism (UNWTO 2013). These global trends require new and different skill and competency sets for present and future tourism workers.

6.4. Tourism Market Competitiveness

Tourism is seen as a driver of economic growth in many countries worldwide. Countries are continuously improving their tourism products to attract visitors to their country. According to Blanke and Chiesa (2013), the aim of travel and tourism competiveness index is to measure the factors and policies that make it attractive to develop tourism and travel sector in different countries. The index is based on three broad categories of regulatory framework, business environment and infrastructure, and human, capital, and national resources. In 2013, the top twelve countries in the Americas are United States, Canada, Barbados, Panama, Mexico, Costa Rica, Brazil, Puerto Rico, Chile, Uruguay, Argentina, and Jamaica.

Jamaica's performance in the competitiveness index is shown in table 6.2. In 2013, Jamaica was ranked 67th out of 140 countries, 65th in 2011, and 60th in 2009. This suggests that Jamaica continues to decline in the competitiveness index.

Table 6.2. Travel and Tourism Competitiveness Index 2013 Ranking for Jamaica

The Travel and Tourism Competitiveness Index	Rank/ (out of 140)	Score (1-7)
2013 Travel and Tourism Competiveness Index	67	4.1
2011 Travel and Tourism Competiveness Index	65	4.1
2009 Travel and Tourism Competitiveness Index	60	4.1
T&T Regulatory Framework	59	4.8
Policy rules and regulations	20	5.1
Environmental sustainability	98	4.3
Safety and security	95	4.3
Health and hygiene	92	4.1
Prioritisation of travel and tourism	7	6.0
Business Environment and Infrastructure	64	3.8
Air transportation infrastructure	63	3.2
Ground transport infrastructure	45	4.3
Tourism infrastructure	59	4.4
ICT infrastructure	92	2.6
Price competitiveness in the T&T industry	95	4.3
T&T Human, Capital, and Natural Resources	87	3.7
Human resource	84	4.7
Education and training	80	4.5
Availability of qualified labour	82	5.0
Affinity for Travel and Tourism	27	5.1
Natural Resources	80	3.4
Cultural Resources	108	1.6

Source: World Economic Forum (2013). *The Travel and Tourism Competitiveness Report 2013: Reducing Barriers to Economic Growth and Job Creation* (p. 208 by J. Blanke and T. Chiesa.

Jamaica was ranked 108th out of 140 countries in cultural resources. This category addresses the number of world heritage sites, sports stadiums, number of international fairs and exhibitions, and creative industries exports. This is an area of concern and must be addressed to increase its performance. The best rank is in prioritisation of travel and tourism, which is 7th out of 140 countries. This category looks at government prioritisation of the industry, government's expenditure, effectiveness of marketing to attract tourists, comprehensiveness, and timeliness of data.

6.5. Market Performance

During the period from 2009 to 2012, the highest number of stopover visitors to Jamaica came from the United States of America, with the highest in 2012, followed by Canada, which grows over the period, as shown in table 6.3. Europe and the Caribbean had a drop in stopover arrivals in 2012. The top four stopover arrivals from the Caribbean countries came from the Cayman Islands, Trinidad and Tobago, Bahamas, and Barbados (JTB 2012). Most visitors from European countries arrived from United Kingdom, Germany, Italy, and France. There had been a drop in stopover arrivals for Latin America and other countries in 2010 but improved in 2011 and 2012. Latin America continues to be a market that has potential for Jamaica. The stopover arrivals from Latin America have improved as a result of doubling of scheduled airlift and visa facilitation.

Table 6.3. Stopover Visitors by Market Share 2009–2012

Countries	Stopover Arrivals (,000)			
	2009	2010	2011	2012
USA	1,172.80	1,242.90	1,225.60	1,257.70
Canada	290.3	325.2	378.9	403.2
Europe	276.8	271.3	253	222.4
Caribbean	65.3	58.3	66.2	65.0
Latin America	14.5	13.4	16.6	25.0
Other Countries	11.3	10.5	11.4	12.8
Total	1,831.00	1,921.60	1,951.70	1,986.10

Source: Jamaica Tourist Board (2012). *Annual Travel statistics, p.5.*

The purpose of visit for most stopover arrivals was for leisure, recreation, and holiday, as shown in table 6.4. The second reason for visiting Jamaica was to visit friends and relatives, which decline in 2011 by 9,616 tourists and increased again in 2012. The third reason was other / not stated, followed by business matters.

Table 6.4. Stopover Arrivals by Purpose of Visit

Purpose of Visit	2009	2010	2011	2012
Leisure, Recreation, and Holiday	1,403,812	1,482,979	1,519,363	1,573,853
Visiting Friends and Relatives	186,265	193,117	183,501	185,646
Business	101,310	102,743	105,839	100,360
Others / Not Stated	139,710	142,839	143,049	126,226
Total	1,831,097	1,921,678	1,951,752	1,986,085

Source: Jamaica Tourist Board (2012). *Annual Travel statistics, p. 36.*

6.6. Role of Government in the Tourism Industry

The government has an important role to play in the tourism industry to ensure its long-term development as it acts as regulator and facilitator through the various agencies, policy, and legislative arrangements (Tourism Sector Plan 2009). The tourism portfolio is the responsibility of the Ministry of Tourism, and its responsibilities include tourism policy, tourism product, marketing and promotion, and travel agencies. The government of Jamaica provides a number of services such as education and training at institutions such as HEART Trust / National Training Agency, Tourism Product Development Company (TPDCo), colleges, universities, and other institutions that are crucial to the development of a competitive workforce. In 2013, the Ministry of Tourism and Entertainment, through the TPDCo, embarked on a language skills training programme aimed at training approximately three hundred sector workers in the tourism industry over a twelve-week period in conversational Russian and Spanish to enable them to better cater to the needs of the target markets (Miller 2013).

The government monitors the progress of strategies such as the Master Plan for Sustainable Tourism Development and Vision 2030, which is Jamaica's National Development Plan. The challenges of competition have led Jamaica to develop tourism development strategies focused on sustainability, productivity, innovation, and competitiveness based on high quality of attractions and services.

According to the Government of Jamaica (2013), during the period 2009–2012, progress made towards the tourism industry includes the completion of Falmouth Cruise Ship Pier and Montego Bay Convention Centre as major tourism projects, expansion in hotel accommodation and attractions, passage of Casino Act 2010 to govern casino gambling, development of draft Community Tourism Policy, Craft Development Strategy, and diversification of the island's tourism source markets. The priority areas for 2012–2015 are development of community-based tourism programmes, further diversification of the tourism market segment, including medical, sports, cultural, and heritage tourism. Marketing strategies continue to be developed for China, Japan, India, and Russia. Strategies are also developed for the South American markets. A study to guide the development of medical tourism in Jamaica and a concept paper on health and wellness are to be completed (PIOJ 2012).

6.7. Master Plan for Sustainable Tourism Development

Jamaica completed a master plan for sustainable tourism development in 2013 (PIOJ 2009). According to the Commonwealth Secretariat (2009), this plan is to move the industry on a path of sustainability and requires the achievement of five main objectives:

1. Increase growth based on sustainable market position based on Jamaica's heritage—natural, cultural, historic.

2. Improve visitor experience by increasing the types and quality of attractions.

3. Community-based development where residents will take ownership of the industry. The local residents must be able to define, develop, and manage the tourism experience within the community.

4. An inclusive industry where people will see tourism as a source of benefit to self and the country.

5. Environmental sustainability where the industry must contribute to the preservation of the natural habitat.

According to the Ministry of Tourism (2012), the Tourism Enhancement Fund (TEF) was established in 2005 to provide financial resources to implement the recommendations of the master plan for sustainable development. There has been progress towards meeting some of the targets in the master plan; however, there are several areas that have not experienced commensurate progress (PIOJ 2009).

6.8. Vision 2030: Jamaica's National Development Plan

According to PIOJ (2009), there is a vision of an inclusive, world-class distinctly Jamaican tourism industry with a well-educated, highly skilled, and motivated workforce at all levels within a safe, secure, and sustainable managed environment. The plan outlines the sector strategies to achieve the vision for the tourism industry. Some of the strategies are as follows:

- Creating a framework that allows awareness, participation, business opportunities, and access for stakeholders

- Developing a dynamic and flexible demand-driven education and training system for tourism and strengthening the social infrastructure of workers and adjoining communities

- Economic integration and development by establishing marketing systems to link the purchasers in the industry and producers in linkage sectors and industries, promoting and enhancing investment opportunities for both local and international investors

- Competitive tourism product by developing new tourism market segment by diversifying the geographic source market and implementing heritage, cultural, historical, and nature-based attraction projects

• Sustainable natural, social, and built environment by ensuring tourism industry activities support biodiversity conservation objectives and compliance with health and safety standards

6.9. Issues and Challenges affecting the Tourism Industry

The economic benefit that flows from the development of tourism is well known, but there are concerns about the negative social and economic impacts of tourism on local people and their communities (Rhiney 2012). Stakeholders are aware that Jamaica faces fierce competition from destinations in Latin America, Asia, Pacific, and Florida and the unpredictable characteristics of the industry. Dodman (2009) discusses (as cited in Nelson 2012), the distribution of benefits from the growth of tourism has not been allocated equally and creates social and environmental problems.

There is a concern that the real economic benefits of tourism are not revealed by gross foreign exchange earnings but what is left after deducting the amount that stays or remains overseas (Gmelch 2012). In the Caribbean, most of the tourism products, which include hotels and tour companies, are foreign owned, and they retain most of the profits (Nelson and Gmelch 2012). The all-inclusive holiday package that covers airfare, accommodation, food, and services that tourists pay for overseas creates another situation where most of the foreign exchange does not reach the Caribbean but the foreign owners' country. Local businesses are affected because tourists remain on the resort and have limited contact with local residents, and this limits most of the spending to the resort itself (Nelson 2012).

According to Rhiney (2012), the high and persistent levels of violent crimes plaguing Jamaica pose a potential threat to the island's tourism product. Although serious crimes against tourists are few, the negative publicity of this problem has implications for visitor arrivals and potential investors to the country. One of the responses to address the issue of visitor safety is developing more large-scale all-inclusive resorts where guests are encouraged to remain on the property. The all-inclusive resort concept is credited for the continued growth of the Jamaican tourism industry even with the island's reputation of having one of the highest crime rates in the world per capita. According to Boxill (2004), as cited in Rhiney (2012), all-inclusive hotels are known to attract visitors as they are promised a safe and secure accommodation. The hotels are protected with highly fenced-off compounds and guarded gates to shield and protect them from the crime problems that exist in the wider Jamaican society. In recent years, the government has had to put measures in place to mitigate the negative publicity of crime in the country by increasing the number of promotional campaigns, exacting fines associated with offences against visitors since 1997, and ensuring that police and courtesy officers are placed in major resort towns.

The growth in the tourism industry has led to inflation of food and land prices (Gmelch 2012). Lands in the vicinity where hotels and tourist facilities are constructed are sold for exorbitant sums, out of the reach of many local people. This results in illegal occupation of land or squatting settlements in these areas. Cummings (2009) defines *squatter settlement* based on a definition by Global Development Research Centre as a residential area that has developed without legal claims to the land and/ or permission from the concerned authorities to build. Tourism attracts employment as it is thought to offer better pay and more consistent employment. As a result, this leads to migration of people close to the resort areas and increase in squatter settlements. This unplanned approach of settlements contributes to health issues as it lacks basic utilities such as running water, sanitary disposal facilities, environmental degradation, and leads to haven for criminals and exposure to hazards.

6.10. Importance of Tourism to Jamaica

6.10.1. Tourism Structure

The industry consists of private and public players in various subsectors, such as accommodations, food and beverage facilities, transportation, in-bound shopping, tourist attractions, and crafts (Tourism Task Force 2009).

- Accommodation is provided at hotels, guest houses, apartments, and resort villas. The all-inclusive and large hotels represent the main type of accommodation. Hotel Incentive and Resort Cottages Incentives Acts provide incentives to encourage the development and improvement in the accommodation sector. A number of properties have changed ownership and are undergoing major refurbishing. These include Memories White Sands, formerly Breezes Trelawny, to be reopened in 2014; Jewel Paradise Cove, formerly Royal Decameron Caribbean; and Wyndam, New Kingston. Food and beverage facilities such as restaurants, pubs, lounges, nightclubs can be included in tourism accommodations or they can stand alone.

- Attractions include ecotourism, recreational and environmental facilities, cultural, historical, and aquatic. The attractions incentives package was approved by the cabinet since 2003 to establish, refurbish, and reposition attractions in an effort to stimulate growth. Tourism Product Development Company monitors the enterprises within this sector.

- The transportation sector is divided into cruise, air, and ground. Air access and internal transportation infrastructures are developed to stimulate economic development. This satisfies tourist needs as well as local population and entrepreneurs for their own businesses. Cruise tourism has grown steadily over the years, as shown in table 6.1. Jamaica continues to record over a million cruise passengers since 2011. Jamaica is served by major cruise companies such as Royal Caribbean Cruises and Carnival Cruise Line. In 2012, *Oasis of the Seas* of the Royal Caribbean Cruises made twenty-six calls to the Port of Falmouth with 154,438 passengers, and *Carnival Magic* of Carnival Cruise Line made thirty-five cruise ship calls to Montego Bay and provided 150,129 cruise passengers. Air transportation allows for access to and within Jamaica. There are developments, such as increase in airlift services, as new airlines and charters have opened new routes and markets that result in increase in tourist arrivals. Ground transportation includes car rental operations, contract carriage operators, transport associations like Jamaica Union of Travellers Association, MAXI, and independent operators.

- There are in-bound shops located within airports, hotels, and shopping centres in the resort areas, and these allow tourists to access duty-free shopping items such as imported luxury goods and souvenir items.

6.10.2. Linkages of Tourism with other Economic Sectors

The economic impact of the tourism sector is significant, although still not fully defined. The tourism industry creates linkages that add value to other economic sectors. Tourism is considered to be a broad service sector that requires a wide range of simple and complex goods and services to support it.

The Tourism Task Force (2009) states that there are numerous examples of linkages between tourism and services and other sectors:

- Agriculture, which remains an important sector in Jamaica. There is a linkage as accommodation subsector is the major user of agricultural products that they procure from large distributors or small contractors. This linkage has potential for local farmers in terms of employment opportunities as long as they can provide the range and quality of products to the tourism sector.

- Manufacturing industry consists of companies that provide food and agro-processing, furniture, chemicals, cosmetic products. The Jamaican manufacturing sector is not very competitive due to high prices and is unable to compete with imports as suppliers to the tourism market.

- Construction in terms of large investments in hotel expansion and development of new hotels. As a result, there is a demand for housing units close to resort areas to cater to workers in the industry.

- Public utilities and infrastructure, including electricity, communications, transportation, and water, are important to the operations of the tourism industry. The liberalisation of the telecommunications sector has provided more access to use of Internet and telephone services. There are concerns about the cost of electricity due to oil prices, and measures to use alternative energy sources have been considered. The upgrading of water and sewage systems is an ongoing concern for authorities.

- Entertainment is one of the vibrant products in the tourism industry and provides opportunity for growth and income generation. It is linked to musical festivals, national and community festivals, and local plays.

The Ministry of Tourism and Entertainment established the Tourism Linkages Council to provide general oversight and guidance on matters related to strengthen existing linkages between tourism and other sectors of the Jamaican economy such as agriculture, manufacturing and entertainment and forge new ones (Ministry of Tourism 2013).

6.10.3. Tourism and Employment

Tourism provides employment for persons in facilities used by tourists such as hotels, tourist attractions and restaurants. It also provides indirect employment and opportunities for self-employment in transportation, agriculture, construction and other service industries (Buckle-Scott, Davis-Morrison, Jaimungalsingh, Lunt 2013).

According to the World Travel and Tourism Council (2013) data shown in table 6.5, there have been fluctuations in travel and tourism's direct contribution to employment. Over the period from 2007 to 2012, the highest number of persons employed in 2007 was 95,500, and the lowest was of 87,700 in 2010. There is an estimate of 94,400 persons to be employed directly in 2013. The total contribution of tourism and travel to employment in Jamaica was 291,900 persons in 2012. The forecast is that this will rise by 5.7 per cent in 2013 to 308,500 jobs (26.1 per cent of total employment). By 2023, travel and tourism is forecasted to support 412,000 jobs (31.4 per cent of total employment), an increase of 2.9 per cent over the period.

Table 6.5. Travel and Tourism Contribution
to Employment from 2007 to 2012

Jamaica	2007	2008	2009	2010	2011	2012	2013 (Estimate)
Travel and Tourism Direct Contribution to Employment							
Real growth (%)	-2.7	-4.0	2.0	-6.2	0.7	1.2	5.5
Thousand (000)	95.5	91.7	93.6	87.7	88.4	89.5	94.4
Travel and Tourism Total Contribution to Employment							
Real growth (%)	-2.2	-5.5	5.6	-3.8	0.9	1.5	5.7
Thousand (000)	297.2	280.6	296.4	284.9	287.5	291.9	308.5

Source: World Travel and Tourism Council (WTTC) (2013). *Travel and Tourism Impact 2013*, pp. 12 and 14.

6.10.4. Contribution to Gross Domestic Product and Foreign Exchange Earnings

Tourism is one of the main foreign exchange earners for the country. When the total visitor arrivals increase, it results in more expenditure of foreign exchange. The country continues to derive most of its foreign exchange from tourism, remittances, and bauxite/alumina. According to WTTC (2013), the direct contribution to GDP in 2012 was US$1.256 billion, which was a 3.6 per cent growth, and projected to be US$1.379 billion in 2013, as shown in table 6.6. This reflects economic activity generated by industries such as hotel, travel agents, airlines, and other passenger transportation services—excluding commuter services. Jamaica is ranked 86th out of 184 countries in terms of total contribution to GDP (WTTC 2013). The total contribution of tourism to GDP was US$4.112 billion in 2012 and is forecasted to rise by 4.2 per cent in 2013 (WTTC 2013).

Table 6.6. Travel and Tourism Direct Contribution to Gross Domestic Product

Jamaica	2007	2008	2009	2010	2011	2012	2013
Travel & Tourism Direct Contribution to GDP							
US$ bn	1.166	1.206	1.128	1.145	1.171	1.256	1.379
Real growth (%)	-3.5	-4.9	1.9	-8.6	-4.4	3.6	4.6
Travel & Tourism Total Contribution to GDP							
US$ bn	3.607	3.678	3.551	3.742	3.846	4.112	4.497
Real growth (%)	-3	-6.3	5.2	-5.1	-3.9	3.2	4.2

Source: World Travel and Tourism Council (WTTC) (2013).

6.11. Importance of TVET in Addressing the Changes in the Jamaican Tourism Industry

The tourism industry is one of the rapidly growing industries in global economy with an increased level of competitiveness among countries to attract visitors to their shores. This industry provides direct employment in institutions that are dedicated to tourism, such as hotels, restaurants, or stores, and indirect employment in areas such as manufacture, construction, agriculture, and entertainment. The advances in technology have resulted in changes in business operations and require skills to produce the quality product that is expected by tourists. Stakeholders in the tourism industry will have to continue educating, training, and retraining their workforce through technical and vocational education and training (TVET) to ensure that it remains competitive. In order to meet the growing demands for skilled workforce, a comprehensive, up-to-date, and effective TVET programme is important. An effective TVET system is important to a country's development as it can increase productivity and reduce poverty, increase levels of education and training support cooperation between private and public sectors, and further develop priority sectors, such as energy and environment (MacDonald, Nink, and Duggan 2010).

According to UNESCO (2004), the revised recommendation defines *technical and vocational education and training* as a comprehensive term referring to those aspects of the educational process involving, in addition to general education, the study of technologies and related sciences and the acquisition of practical skills, attitudes, and understanding and knowledge related to occupations in various sectors of economic and social life. It also prepares persons for lifelong learning and promotes environmentally sound, sustainable development that is important to tourism industry. These knowledge, skills, and attitudes are important to the tourism industry, and TVET itself has to change to meet these changes in development.

Charles (2002) suggests the following skills and competencies required based on trends in the tourism industry:

1. Entrepreneurial and intrapreneurial skills and competencies that prepare persons to create business and employment opportunities for themselves or for the organisations with which they work. Creativity and innovation are important components to entrepreneurship, as tourism demands changes. This requires persons who can develop new approaches to attract tourists to different destinations.

2. Information technological skills for all levels of jobs, from the room attendant who may be faced with 'smart,' self-cleaning rooms or handheld computers to communicate with the stockroom or laundry to the vendor at the beach who may have to accept credit cards.

3. Environmental awareness and ethics skills as tourism workers will have to appreciate the issues associated with sustaining tourism. There are new tourism products, such as ecotourism and cultural tourism, emerging that require tourism workers to have technical and conceptual skills to work in these areas.

4. New management skills and competencies such as systems thinking, environmental scanning, visioning the future before it happens. The future tourism manager should be a learner and must continuously update his or her skills and competencies.

5. Behavioural skills such as communication, interpersonal relations, customer service, proper work ethic, and positivity are of critical importance. Recruitment of future tourism workers will be as important as proper training and development opportunities.

6.12. Current State of TVET in Preparing Jamaicans for the Tourism Industry

6.12.1. Formal Education System

The formal education system in Jamaica has four levels, namely, early childhood, primary, secondary, and tertiary (Ministry of Education 2013a). The government is responsible for the education sector; however, a small level of private sector participation exists. Students are introduced to TVET programmes at the secondary level primarily at the upgraded high schools, where more emphasis is placed on technical and vocational education when compared with traditional high schools (Harris 2009). The technical and vocational education unit in the Ministry of Education monitors the technical and vocational programme in schools through five areas: agriculture, business education, home economics, industrial education, and visual arts (MOE, n.d.). Secondary level education is offered in two cycles. The first cycle is three years and is provided at grades 7–9, and the second cycle is for years, grades 10 and 11. Students are expected to sit the Caribbean Examination Council's Caribbean Secondary Education Certificate (CSEC) at the end of the grade 11. Some institutions offer a further two years (grades 12 and 13) that allow students to pursue the Caribbean Advanced Proficiency Examinations (CAPE). CAPE is designed to provide certification of the academic, vocational, and technical achievement of students. Also, some high schools have a continuing education programme, provided under the Career Advancement Programme (CAP), which is a youth career development and education initiative developed by the Ministry of Education and its agency HEART / Trust NTA.

Tertiary level education is offered to students who have successfully completed secondary education and who desire pursuing further studies. Training and workforce development programmes are offered at the tertiary level to prepare persons for the tourism industry. Advanced programmes are offered at the University of the West Indies, Mona, and the University of Technology, Jamaica. Other institutions such as teachers' and community colleges offer specialised programmes. Institutions that prepare students directly or indirectly for the tourism industry are College of Agriculture, Science, and Education and Edna Manley College of the Visual and Performing Arts. Private institutions such as the Northern Caribbean University and the University College of the Caribbean offer degrees in education, science, and technology.

6.12.2. HEART Trust / National Training Agency

The Human Employment and Resource Training (HEART) Trust / National Training Agency (NTA) is a statutory agency of the Ministry of Education. It was established under the Human Employment and Resource Training Act of 1982. The Trust finances and coordinates training programmes with the objective of creating a competitive workforce consistent with the needs of the labour market according to international standards. According to HEART/NTA (2011), the operational plan is focused on training for capacity building in sectors including tourism and agriculture, which have been tagged as strategic areas for national growth and development in the Vision 2030 plan. Learners can access training programmes at workforce colleges, TVET institutes, and community training partnerships and on-the-job training through the Registered Apprenticeship Programme (RAP) and the School Leavers Training Opportunities Programme (SLTOP). These programmes are geared towards transforming the lives of school leavers as well as employed persons who require training and certification. HEART Trust / NTA training model uses the competency-based approach. Trainees are expected to demonstrate the tasks associated with a particular set of competency standards. Competency-based education and training (CBET) has the capacity to reduce the gap between the school system and labour market as persons are certified based on demonstrating the skills outline in the occupational standards. This training has to be accessed in a training environment, either in the institution or in the industry. According to McLean (2011), countries such as Europe, Asia, Australia, and South America have adopted CBET for training and assessment as it is necessary for the continuous provision of skilled labour in the workforce. They are expected to demonstrate this in an assessment session. Trainees are expected to transfer and apply the skills learnt in training to meet new challenges and situations.

According to HEART (n.d.) the HEART Trust / NTA has been responding to the growing and changing demand for skills in tourism. This agency has increased its offerings in tourism, especially in hospitality. However, there is a need for higher-level training programmes. There are initiatives to rebrand the institutions—for example, Runaway Bay HEART Hotel in St. Ann has become the Cardiff Hotel and Spa and is positioned to become a four-star hotel; Kenilworth Academy in Hanover to be called HEART College of Tourism and Recreation; and Ebony Park Academy in Clarendon to be called HEART College of Agriculture and Ecological Sciences—so that HEART will become a major driver in providing persons for the tourism industry. The introduction of the integrated training system will pave the way for this agency to respond to the competitive economic environment. This system will provide delivery of higher-quality programmes, opportunity for industry-based training through productive enterprises, and fostering the development and growth of micro, small, and medium enterprises through an incubator experience. One central feature of this system is the development of workforce colleges and TVET institutes. TVET institutes comprise clusters of existing HEART institutions in a manner that improves efficiency by region. The rebranded HEART institutions will deliver training with little or no classroom theoretical sessions through more multimedia interactions and more emphasis on experimentation, the development of entrepreneurial skills, and internship (Morris 2011). Workforce colleges will offer higher-level experiential programmes at level 5. TVET institutes will focus on levels 3 and 4 while offering selected levels 1 and 2 programmes.

6.12.3. Integration of TVET in the Formal Education System

The Ministry of Education has proposed plans to integrate TVET in the formal education system. According to McLean (2012), the TVET policy proposes that students are exposed to career awareness (grades k–6), career exploration (grades 7–9), career preparation and development (grades 10–11), and career advancement programme (grades 12–13). Students should be exposed at the secondary level workplace experience through school-based apprenticeship. Curriculum reform at the grades 7–9 level includes the resource and technology programme in all schools. The programme will include problem-solving methodology, creating innovations within real-life situations, among other interesting features. This programme will better prepare students for TVET at the upper secondary level. In addition to CSEC, students at the grades 10 and 11 level will be prepared for certification with the National Vocational Qualifications (Jamaica and the Caribbean Vocational Qualifications). The career-advancement programme (CAP) is an expanded education and training programme that places students in a career path and certifies them for employment (Ministry of Education 2013c).

In order to accomplish integration of TVET in the formal education system, TVET professionals should be trained in leadership and methodologies of competency-based education and training (CBET). Competency-based training programmes comprise competency standards set by the industry against which students are assessed to ensure all the outcomes required have been achieved. Some high school laboratories and workshops will be upgraded to enable them to improve their offering of levels 1 and 2 in technical and vocational subject areas (Ministry of Education 2013c).

6.13. Challenges in the TVET System

6.13.1. CSEC Performance

Performance of students in CSEC mathematics and English A is an area of concern as Jamaica moves towards knowledge-based society. Students are expected to pass these core subjects along with a TVET subject area to prepare them for further training. Table 6.7 shows the performance of Jamaican public school candidates in 2012 and 2013 in the CSEC examinations. A comparison of the percentage of persons attaining grades 1, 2, and 3 in 2012 and 2013 reveals that there was an 11.7 per cent increase in English A and 4.7 per cent in mathematics. Technical/vocational and business subjects are performing above the core subjects of mathematics and English A with an average passing rate of over 80 per cent. The core subjects for matriculation to tertiary level institutions are mathematics and English A. Of the grade 11 cohort of 42,200 students, only 26,489 or 62.7 per cent sat English A and 22,870 or 54.2 per cent sat mathematics. Therefore, the training system continues to be negatively affected by problems in the secondary schools as students are leaving without the prerequisite subjects.

Table 6.7. Performance of Public School Candidates Performance in 2012 and 2013 CSEC Examination

Subject	2013		2012	
	No. Sitting ,000	Percentage Attaining Grades 1–3*	No. Sitting ,000	Percentage Attaining Grades 1–3*
English A	26.48	63.7	27.63	52.0
Mathematics	22.87	42.2	23.73	37.5
Technical/Vocational	43.93	82.6	43.63	80.7
Agricultural Science (Double and Single Award), Building Technology (Construction and Wood), Clothing and Textiles, Electrical and Electronic Tech, Electronic Document Preparation Management, Food and Nutrition, Home Economics Management, Information Technology, Physical Education and Sports Technical Drawing, Theatre Arts, Visual Arts				
Business	19.73	84.0	211.57	76.3
Economics, Office Administration, Principles of Accounts, Principles of Business				

*Percentage attainment is based on the number of students who sat the examination

Source: Ministry of Education (2013c). Caribbean Secondary Education Certificate 2013 Analysis of the public school's performance.

6.13.2. Financing of TVET

According to PIOJ (2013) in the Vision 2030 Jamaica update, 24.2 per cent of the total labour force has vocational or professional certification based on the quarterly labour force survey for April 2013. This is an increase of 1.6 percentage points from 22.6 per cent in the April 2012 survey. This means that over 70 per cent of the labour force is untrained and the level of funding available is inadequate to finance the training required. TVET is financed through the HEART Trust Fund. The trust is financed by 3 per cent levy on all employers above a given threshold. This fund supports the training activities of the HEART Trust and finances the activities of the National Council on Technical and Vocational Education and Training (NCTVET), which is responsible for developing occupational standards, assessing and awarding the National Vocational Qualification of Jamaica (NVQ-J), accrediting formal, non-formal, and informal TVET programmes. There are established guidelines to finance TVET programmes operated directly by HEART/NTA as well as programmes operated by institutions including community, non-governmental, and private organisations. In the public schools, TVET is financed mostly by the government and, to a lesser extent, private sectors.

According to UNESCO (2004), government and private sector should recognise that TVET is an investment and not a cost with significant returns in providing a competitive workforce; consequently, funding should be shared between government, industry, community, and the learner, with the government providing appropriate financial incentives. Partnerships with employers and training providers need to be stressed as there is a continuing problem of financing the high cost of sustaining the TVET programme due to maintenance and provision of training materials and equipment.

6.13.3. Qualifications Framework

According to PIOJ (2009), Jamaica will create a single national qualifications framework to integrate all qualifications across the education and training systems in terms of content and complexity to establish equivalencies. This will ensure that all training programmes in Jamaica conform to established global standards and provide recognition and credit for previous knowledge and skills. The NCTVET is the local body responsible for assessing and awarding the NVQ-J. Certificates of competence are issued in one of five levels based on completion of the requirements of the training programme. Programmes at the tertiary level have different certification schemes, such as those accredited by the University Council of Jamaica (UCJ) and the Council of Community Colleges of Jamaica (CCCJ). The industry plays an important role in the setting of occupational and competency standards and is crucial to the national qualifications framework (MacDonald, Nink, and Duggan 2010). Stakeholders will have to buy into this new qualifications framework so that learners will be accepted based on qualifications they received as it matches international standards. Employers will accept the qualifications as the training the learners received is of a certain standard and calibre. Technical and vocational education should link with other education sectors to facilitate flexible pathways at all levels so that learners can progress to higher levels of education as part of the lifelong process (UNESCO 2004).

6.13.4. Implementing Caribbean Vocational Qualifications in Education System

In order to remain competitive within the Caribbean Single Market and Economy (CSME), CARICOM states to subscribe to the regional process for workforce training assessment and certification leading to the award of the Caribbean Vocational Qualification (CVQ), and its implementation can be seen as a catalyst for TVET reform (Whiteman 2011). Systems have to be reformed in order to provide a competency-based education and training (CBET) approach to TVET, which is demand-driven and based on occupational standards developed in partnership with the industry. The occupational standards represent current best practices that are relevant to the industry in which the Caribbean Examination Council awards CVQ in the secondary school system for students from fourth year or persons seeking to certify or learn new skills.

Eastmond (2011) identifies some issues and challenges affecting the implementation of CVQ in the Caribbean. First, there is an absence of policies from various ministries of education with respect to the implementation and expansion of CVQs in secondary schools. School administrators and parents select CVQ for students who are less able academically; as such, there is a stigma that TVET qualifications are inferior. Secondly, the quality of teaching in these programmes is considered inferior. There is a lack of buy-in from teachers since they have lost the passion for teaching as a result of factors such as the negative stigma and low status associated with TVET. Additionally, CVQ is an evidence-based approach that requires meticulous record-keeping. Many teachers consider this additional work that they are not prepared to undertake. In general, access to TVET programmes by teachers is limited in the region. This is a dilemma since they require training and certification before they are permitted to teach in the programmes. There is also an issue with the time for training, since teachers are unable to access training programmes during regular school hours and some are unwilling to do this after school and/or during the holiday periods.

Thirdly, schools are required to carry out training using industry standards; consequently, they are forced to employ more flexible schedules that allow students to be exposed to work-based learning since they do not have industry standard equipment, nor do they have access to many industry sites. Additionally, schools within the region and country face resource problems. Equipment, in many cases, is outdated and not operational. These factors can affect the validity of the qualification, especially if the quality assurance procedures and facility standards are not sound. Teachers need support in the implementation of programme especially during the first cycle in terms of completing the various evidence-gathering forms and understanding how to deliver the curriculum. Some countries have few education or curriculum officers who specialise in TVET, and as such, the support for TVET teachers is compromised.

6.13.5. Misalignment of Training Programmes with Labour Market Needs

PIOJ (2009) states the following in Vision 2030: Jamaica National Development Plan:

> Training is often not relevant to new demands and is inadequate in some cases to quickly address the changing needs in the workplace. More emphasis needs to be placed on training for job growth especially in the areas of hospitality, construction, and information communications technology. (p. 65)

There is a need for a system in place to develop mechanism that can identify current and future skills so that TVET programmes can address them. Greater linkages are needed between training institutions and private sector in the development and delivery of programmes (PIOJ 2009). HEART Trust / NTA continually collects and reviews labour information, and the findings are distributed to its institutions to guide their programme design delivery (PIOJ 2012). According to the Jamaica National Report on TVET compiled by HEART Trust / NTA, 'tertiary education programmes are in need of increased relevance to labour market with emphasis on competencies and performance' (p.25).

6.13.6. Role of Stakeholders in TVET

Although there are efforts by HEART Trust / NTA to train and certify approximately one hundred thousand persons per year, this effort alone will not be adequate to upskill the workforce (Hutton 2009). Hutton (2009) suggests that companies and individuals should register for programmes available at private providers and tertiary institutions for equipping the workforce with the required competencies. Tourism is a dynamic industry; therefore, the changes will have an impact on how the workforce can meet the new demands, especially in technical skills. Sandals Corporate University was formed to provide opportunities for team members to further their education through on-the-job training and partnerships with renowned universities and colleges ('No Sophomore Slump for Sandals Corporate University', 2013). Adam Stewart, chief executive officer of Sandals Resorts International, said, 'It is impossible to deliver exceptional quality service if you are not equipped with the attitude, skill and knowledge to do so'. According to Ford-Warner (2006), 'small enterprises however tend to place emphasis on training, either because of a lack of financial or human resources, or lack of interest on the part of the owner/ manager' (p. 100).

TPDCo has a partnership with HEART Trust / NTA in financing training in Team Jamaica. This collaboration in 2004 has increased the participation from 1,200 to approximately 7,000 participants per year (Tourism Taskforce 2009). The objective of the Team Jamaica programme is to develop and implement a standardised compulsory training programme for persons who work directly in the tourism sector and interface with tourists at all levels. The components of the programme are customer service, product knowledge, Jamaica's history and geography, and environmental awareness through face-to-face instruction and group interactions (Howell-Williams and Haye 2006). Stakeholders must facilitate work experience programmes so that trainees can be exposed to industry best practices and get a better understanding of the general workplace and the importance of customer service. Training requires collaboration and coordination with employers to address the changes in the workplace. There will be need for on-the-job training to build upon existing abilities and provide learning opportunities to acquire new competencies.

6.14. Recommendations

Based on the issues and challenges identified in the TVET system and tourism industry, the following recommendation should assist in addressing the deficiencies:

1. TVET system must promote a culture of entrepreneurship. Jamaicans will be expected to demonstrate skills in entrepreneurship to develop business and employment opportunities for the country. Jamaica continues to diversify its tourism products to include community tourism. This will require persons to develop products to attract tourists to the community. There is an attempt by HEART Trust / NTA to set up workforce colleges to provide services for small and medium enterprises. However, there is a need for a standard to be established for all institutions that offer vocational programmes to prospective and present entrepreneurs.

2. Education system needs to continue its transformation so that it will become a norm for every single Jamaican to receive at least a solid secondary education. This means that the primary education system must provide the foundation for learning. Secondary schools are expected to build upon the foundation to equip students to acquire advanced knowledge, skills, and attitude, including TVET. It is important that education programmes including TVET should develop students' 'soft skills' so that they can develop personal qualities such as team work, punctuality, initiatives, etc., to work in a dynamic workforce. These skills are important in the tourism and hospitality industry to provide quality service to the tourists.

3. TVET must improve its relevance by advancing the 'greening TVET' agenda to address environmental issues. There are new employment opportunities available

through the ecotourism as another type of tourism product and measures to protect the environment. Stakeholders are aware that tourists are becoming environmentally aware. There are tourism products that depend on natural resources. Tourism has negative impacts on the environment, and as a result, environmental monitoring, recycling, alternative energy sources, pollution control, waste management, and other measures need to be implemented. Greening TVET is important to ensure the sustainability of our environment as there are tourism products that depend on natural resources.

4. TVET must be given equal status as general education and must be made available in the formal education system. This requires a marketing campaign to improve TVET status to parents, teachers, and students as it prepares persons for the world of work and its contribution to economic development. Successful persons in the TVET field must become ambassadors to promote TVET in schools through speeches, visits, and media campaigns to motivate persons on the importance of this form of education to national development. The preparation of the national qualifications framework must continue to involve stakeholders so that they will associate themselves with it during implementation. This will improve the status of TVET as learners progress from one stage of certification to another.

5. The promotion of competency-based education and training (CBET) and implementation of the Caribbean Vocational Qualifications (CVQ) to the education system must continue as this will address the needs of the workforce. Training of TVET instructors/teachers must continue in the utilisation of CBET especially in the secondary schools as this approach will be new to those who are currently in the teaching profession. The

Caribbean Examination Council (CXC) must promote CVQ certification in high schools by continuing to engage the stakeholders in education and industry to support this vocational qualification. CXC can review the technical/ vocational subjects offered and utilise the CBET approach in the curriculum in assessing the school-based assessment skills. Also, students completing certain sections of the syllabus should be certified with a CVQ certification.

6. There is a need for more partnerships between education and training institutions and industries in the country. Financing for TVET is an expensive investment as technology changes, hence the need to upgrade facilities to match the needs of industry. Industries can adopt a school and provide financial resources through sponsorship or donations to ensure that the TVET programme runs effectively. Through partnerships, TVET will be able to provide the educational and training needs to satisfy unmet demands. This will reduce the misalignment of labour needs to training provided. TVET system should have continuous collection of labour market information from employers so that steps can be put in place to either remove, revamp, or add a new course to address the changes in the market.

7. There is a need for new foreign language training as the Jamaican government continues to diversify its market to attract tourists from countries such as Russia and China. In addition to providing foreign language training, present and prospective workers in the tourism industry need to understand the culture of these persons to be able to cater to their needs. The use of short courses to acquaint current workforce in new languages must continue. However, students pursuing courses in tourism and hospitality and prospective entrepreneurs must be exposed to the different languages starting at the high school level. A major

challenge would be the availability of language teachers to provide training in all languages in schools. A possible solution is to establish linkages with institutions that can offer these languages to the tourism and hospitality trainees.

6.15. Conclusion

The tourism and hospitality industry has been growing significantly over the years and is predicted to continue doing so. It is important to the Jamaican economy and is one of the main sources of foreign exchange and employment. The Jamaican economy is primarily a service economy. In order to compete effectively in a service economy, it is important to improve human capital. This service industry requires a workforce that is competent and is able to improve the tourism product in the country.

CTVET plays an important role in preparing the present and future workforce for the changes occurring in the tourism industry. However, there are challenges in the current TVET system. The challenges are unsatisfactory performance in core subjects, misalignment of labour market needs with training, lack of financial resources, and lack of integration of TVET in the education system. These issues must be addressed in order to have an effective TVET system.

An attempt has been made by the government of Jamaica and other stakeholders in preparing Vision 2030: Jamaica National Development Plan document to improve tourism and education and training systems in the country. Stakeholders should ensure that this plan is implemented. It is important to sustain and improve the collaboration and partnership between various stakeholders and the education and training systems to ensure that the above recommendations are considered and possibly implemented to address the challenges affecting the tourism industry.

Halden A. Morris

6.16. References

Blanke, J, and Chiesa T., eds. 2013. 'The Travel and Tourism Competiveness Report 2013: Reducing Barriers to Economic Growth and Job Creation'. World Economic Forum. Retrieved from http://www3.weforum.org/docs/ WEF_TT_Competitiveness_Report_2013.pdf.

Boxhill, I. 2004. 'Towards an Alternative Tourism for Jamaica'. *International Journal of Contemporary Hospitality Management* 16 (4), 269–272. doi: 10.1108/09596110410537432.

Buckle-Scott, L., V. Davis-Morrison, and A. Jaimungalsingh. 2013. *Social Studies for CSEC*. Nelson Thornes.

Charles, K. 2002. 'Future Human Resource Development Needs of the Caribbean Tourism Industry'. In *Tourism and Hospitality Education and Training in the Caribbean*. University of the West Indies: 139–152.

Commonwealth Secretariat. 2002. 'Master Plan for Sustainable Tourism Development—Jamaica'. Retrieved on 30 November 2013 from http://www.jtbonline.org/tourism_jamaica/Major%20 Tourism%20Laws/Tourism%20Master%20Plan%20Full.pdf.

Cummings, V. 2009. 'The Problem of Squatting in Jamaica'. *Jamaica Gleaner*. Retrieved from http://jamaica-gleaner.com/ gleaner/20090524/news/news1.html.

Eastmond, H. 2011. 'Issues and Challenges in the Implementation of the CVQ in the Caribbean'. *The Caribbean Examiner* 9 (1): 22–25.

Ford-Warner, K. 2006. 'Challenges to Growth in the Caribbean Tourism Industry: The Education and Training of Our Tourism

248

Workforce. In *Tourism: The Driver of Change in the Jamaican Economy*: 93–102. Retrieved from Caribbean Search database.

Government of Jamaica. 2013. 'Vision 2030: Jamaica National Development Plan' (draft). Medium-Term Socio-Economic Policy Framework 2012–2015. Retrieved from http://www.vision2030.gov.jm/Portals/0/Workshops_Reports/Vision%202030%20Jamaica%20-%20Draft%20MTF%202012-2015%20%28February%202013%29.pdf.

Gmelch, G. 2012. *Behind the Smile: The Working Lives of Caribbean Tourism*, 2nd edition. Indiana University Press.

Harris, B. 2009. 'Attitudes Towards TVET Placement and Implications for Career Choices: A Study of Grade 11 Students in Two High Schools'. *Caribbean Journal of Education* 31 (1): 102–129.

HEART Trust / NTA. n.d. 'Jamaica National Report on Technical and Vocational Education and Training'. Retrieved from http://www.ilocarib.org.tt/cef/national%20employment%20reports/Jamaica%20Nat%20TVET%20Finalreport.pdf.

———. 2011. Annual Report 2010–2011. Kingston, Jamaica. Author.

Howell-Williams, V., and A. Haye, eds. 2006. *Team Jamaica Handbook*, 3rd edition. Tourism Product Development Company.

Hutton, D. 2009. 'Preparing the Workplace for the 21st Century'. *Caribbean Journal of Education* 31 (1): 21–45.

Jamaica Observer. 2013. 'No Sophomore Slump for Sandals Corporate University'. Retrieved from http://www.jamaicaobserver.com/magazines/career/

No-sophomore-slump-for-Sandals-Corporate-University_14970394#ixzz2o4YrYOf9.

Jamaica Tourist Board. n.d. 'Tourism in Jamaica'. Retrieved from http://jtbonline.org/tourism_jamaica/Pages/Introduction.aspxn.

———. 2012. 'Annual Travel Statistics'. Retrieved from http://www.jtbonline.org/statistics/Annual%20Travel/Annual%20Travel%20Statistics%202012.pdf.

MacDonald, S., C. Nink, and S. Duggan. 2010. 'Principles and Strategies of a Successful TVET Program'. Management Training Corporation Institute. Retrieved from http://www.mtctrains.com/public/uploads/1/2011/11/International_TVET_2010.pdf.

McLean, G. 2011. 'Competency-Based Education Training and Assessment: The Pathway to Economic Growth in the Caribbean'. *The Caribbean Examiner* 9 (1): 11–12.

———. 2012. 'Integration of TVET in the Formal Education System: The Case of Jamaica'. Caribbean Conference on TVET. Retrieved from http://www.soeconferences.com/content/integration-tvet-formal-education-system-case-jamaica.

Miller, B. 2013. 'Language Skills Training Programme for Tourism Workers'. Jamaica Information Service. Retrieved from http://jis.gov.jm/language-skills-training-programme-tourism-workers/.

Ministry of Education. 2013a. 'Education Statistics 2012–2013'. Retrieved from http://www.moe.gov.jm/sites/default/files/Education%20Statistics%202012-13.pdf.

———. 2013b. 'Caribbean Secondary Education Certificate 2013 Analysis of the Public School's Performance'. Retrieved from

http://www.moe.gov.jm/sites/default/files/2013%20CSEC%20
Report.pdf.

————. 2013c. 'TVET Qualification Increases Employability'. News
Release. Retrieved from http://www.moe.gov.jm/sites/default/
files/TVET%20Qualification%20Increases%20Employability.pdf.

————. n.d. 'Technical and Vocational Education Unit'. Retrieved
from http://www.moe.gov.jm/node/51.

Ministry of Tourism. 2012. 'Tourism Enhancement Fund'.
Retrieved from http://www.mot.gov.jm/content/
tourism-enhancement-fund.

————. 2013. 'Tourism Linkages Hub'. Retrieved from http://www.
mot.gov.jm/content/tourism-linkages-hub.

Morris, A. 2011. 'HEART Trust Rebrands Institution'. *Jamaica
Observer* (17 April 2011). Retrieved from http://
www.jamaicaobserver.com/magazines/career/
HEART-Trust-rebrands-institutions_8611233.

Morris, H. A. 2013. 'Current Options for Economic Transformation
and Sustainable Job Creation: Internal Action'. Chapter in *The
Integrationist: Economic Transformation and Job Creation—
The Caribbean Experience*. Edited by K. Hall and M. Chuck-A-
Sang. Bloomington: Trafford Publishers.

Nelson, L. 2012. 'Realizing Necessary Positive Changes in
Caribbean Tourism'. *Palermo Business Review*, special issue:
9–27. Retrieved on 29 November 2013 from http://www.
palermo.edu/economicas//PDF_2012/PBR6/PBR-edicion-
especial-01.pdf.

Planning Institute of Jamaica (PIOJ). 2009. 'Vision 2030: Jamaica National Development Plan'. Kingston, Jamaica.

———. 2012. 'Vision 2030: Jamaica National Development Plan— Medium Term Socio-Economic Policy Framework 2009–2012, Two-Year Progress Report, April 2009–March 2011 (draft)'. Retrieved from http://www.vision2030.gov.jm/Portals/0/ Workshops_Reports/MTF%202-Year%20Progress%20Report%20 %28Draft%20-%20February%202012%29.pdf.

———. 2013. 'Vision 2030: Jamaica Update' 6 (3). Retrieved on 2 December 2013 from http://pioj.gov.jm/Portals/0/Social_Sector/ NEWSLETTER%20JULY-SEPT%202013.pdf.

Rhiney, K. 2012. 'The Negril Tourism Industry: Growth, Challenges and Future Prospects'. *Caribbean Journal of Earth Science* 43: 25–34. Retrieved on 30 November 2013 from http://www.mona. uwi.edu/geoggeol/JamGeolSoc/CJES%20Web%20page/ CJESpdf/CJES%2043-04-RhineyNegril.pdf.

Taylor, F. 1993. *To Hell with Paradise: A History of the Jamaican Tourist Industry*. University of Pittsburgh Press.

Tourism Task Force. 2009. 'Vision 2030: Tourism Sector Plan 2009– 2030'. Retrieved on 30 November 2013 from http://www. dawgen.com/blog/wp-content/uploads/2013/03/Microsoft-Word-Vision-2030-Jamaica-Final-Draft-Tourism-Sector-Plan-_Sep%C3%A2%E2%82%AC%C2%A6.pdf.

UNESCO. 2004. 'Normative Instruments Concerning Technical and Vocational Education'. Retrieved on 21 September 2013 from http://unesdoc.unesco.org/images/0014/001406/140603e.pdf.

UNWTO.n.d. 'Understanding Tourism: Basic Glossary'. Retrieved on 30 November 2013 from http://media.unwto.org/en/content/understanding-tourism-basic-glossary.

———. 2013. 'Annual Report 2012'. Retrieved on 25 November 2013 from http://dtxtq4w60xqpw.cloudfront.net/sites/all/files/pdf/annual_report_2012.pdf.

Whiteman, P. 2011. 'The Caribbean Vocational Qualification (CVQ)'. *The Caribbean Examiner* 9 (1): 14–15.

World Travel and Tourism Council (WTTC). 2013. 'Travel and Tourism Economic Impact 2013'. Retrieved from http://www.wttc.org/site_media/uploads/downloads/jamaica2013_1.pdf.

Zappino, V. 2005. 'Caribbean Tourism and Development: An Overview'. (ECDPM Discussion Paper No. 65). Maastricht: ECDPM. Retrieved from http://www.ecdpm.org/Web_ECDPM/Web/Content/Content.nsf/0/1e3d9756d36aa3b4c125703c004f2eb6?OpenDocument#sthash.waYAHQTE.dpuf.

APPENDICES

APPENDIX 4.1: **REGIONAL FIVE - LEVEL QUALIFICATIONS FRAMEWORK**

Type/Level of Program	Orientation And Purpose	Credits	Entry Requirements	Occupational Competence	Academic Competence
Level 1/ Certificate	Completion of a preparatory programme leading to further study in a given academic or vocational area or entry qualification for a particular occupation	Minimum 10 Credits	To be determined by the local training Institution	Semi-skilled, entry level. Supervised worker	Grade 10
Level 2/ Certificate	To prepare a skilled independent worker who is capable of study at the next level (post-secondary)	Minimum 20 Credits	Grade 11 or Equivalent	Skilled Worker Unsupervised Worker	Grade 11
Level 3/ Diploma and Associate Degree	A post-secondary qualification emphasising the acquisition of knowledge, skills and attitudes (behavioural competencies) to function at the technician/supervisory level and pursue studies at a higher level.	Diploma: Minimum 50 Credits Associate Degree: Minimum 60 Credits	4 CXCs, Level 2 Certification or Equivalent	Technician, Supervisory	Associate Degree Entry to Bachelor's Degree programme with or without advanced standing
Level 4/ Bachelor's Degree	Denoting the acquisition of an academic, vocational, professional qualification, who can create, design and maintain systems based on professional expertise	Minimum 120 Credits	5 CXC's, Level 3 Certification or Equivalent	Competence which involves the application of knowledge in a broad range of complex, technical or professional work activities performed in a wide range of contexts. This includes Master Craftsman, Technologists, Advanced Instructor, Manager, Entrepreneur	
Level 5/ Post Graduate/ Advanced Professional	Denoting the acquisition of advanced professional post-graduate Competence in specialized field of study or occupation.		Level 4 Certification or Equivalent	Competence which involves the application of a range of fundamental principles at the level of chartered, advanced professional and senior management occupations.	

Dunn-Smith P. (2006)

APPENDIX 4.2: **CARIBBEAN QUALIFICATIONS FRAMEWORK (DRAFT II)**

Qualification Levels [Cumulative]	Knowledge [Theoretical & factual]	Skills & application [Cognitive, practical & communication skills and the context for their application]	Autonomy and responsibility [including team role]
I	Elementary general knowledge of a field of work or study	**Skills:** Elementary general, logical and practical skills **Type of activity/ Context:** Routine, repetitive situations **Communication:** Read and write limited types and lengths of materials; understand and follow simple instructions; identify and report facts.	Needs direct supervision and detailed guidance to complete routine, repetitive tasks.
II	Foundational factual and operational knowledge of a field of work or study	**Skills:** Foundational, logical and practical skills **Type of activity/ Context:** Defined, routine, structured **Communication:** Extract information from specified range of sources; produce simple written documents using templates; take part in discussion.	Needs some supervision and clear instructions in order to perform on structured assignments and achieve set goals.
III	Knowledge and understanding of, and ability to, apply foundational facts, principles and established processes of a field of work or study	**Skills:** Fundamental logical, and practical skills **Type of activity/ Context:** Defined, non-routine but predictable assignments and contexts **Communication:** Extract information from range of sources; summarize information in written or graphical format; take active part in discussion.	Can accept responsibility for completing assignments provided that goals are outlined. Can implement decisions with limited to no supervision; can help guide/supervise others in simple undertakings.
IV	Core knowledge and understanding of concepts, rules and processes of a field of work or study	**Skills:** Defined range of logical, intuitive and practical skills **Type of activity/ Context:** Non-routine and unpredictable assignments and contexts **Communication:** Summarize research findings using appropriate formats and registers; provide status reports in appropriate formats; take informed position in discussion.	Can work autonomously with limited supervision or guidance; can supervise others in undertaking tasks; take responsibility for organizing self and others once objectives are known; comfortable taking decisions of a routine nature and appropriately escalating more complex challenges.
V	Comprehensive knowledge and understanding of general and specialized areas of a field of work or study	**Skills:** Broad range of logical, intuitive and practical skills **Type of activity/ Context:** Complex assignments in wide range of contexts **Communication:** Develop and communicate plans; analyse and synthesize information from range of sources; transmit information and skills to teams using appropriate formats; lead discussions	Autonomous worker capable of multi-tasking, team supervisor; can adapt behavior and methods; comfortable investigating and solving problems, making process improvements and contributing ideas before escalating more complex challenges; capable of coordinating and/or managing multiple assignments.
VI	Advanced knowledge and understanding of theories, rules, processes, understanding of the limits and having the ability to integrate knowledge	**Skills:** Comprehensive range of logical, intuitive and practical skills **Type of activity/ Context:** Requiring design of solutions in broad range of unfamiliar contexts **Communication:** Communicate improvement plans and designs; prepare technical proposals and research reports; mediate discussions with specialists audiences.	Able to manage multiple, complex assignments in overlapping areas; applies intellectual knowledge and skills to solve problems, design solutions, or improve processes; sets and takes responsibility for meeting goals, team leader.
VII	Very specialized knowledge of a field of work or study with ability to critique and engage in research and contribute to deeper understanding of the areas of specialization	**Skills:** Expert and specialized logical, intuitive and practical skills to solve complex problems **Type of activity/ Context:** Requiring research to devise solutions in related areas **Communication:** Communicate research findings, prepare and present instructional materials to specialists; mediate discussions with specialist and non-specialist audiences; make presentations for advocacy.	Transforms processes and develops new models and theories to improve organization or field of study; self directed, senior team leader, expects responsibility, sets strategic direction; excellent decision maker.
VIII	Specialized knowledge in the forefront of the given field or areas of work and those related to it. Able to make original contributions to knowledge	**Skills:** Specialized skills logical, intuitive and practical skills to work autonomously create ground breaking solutions. **Type of activity/Context:** Requiring innovation to develop original solutions and new procedures for current and anticipated situations. **Communication:** Publish technical and academic materials for peers and the community; make presentations for advocacy functions	Innovative and transformational decision-maker and leader; prefers independent and autonomous working style; defines groundbreaking models and theories for system improvement.

Wright, Y (2012)

ABBREVIATIONS

AACs	Australian Apprenticeship Centres
ANTA	Australian National Training Authority
AQF	Australian Qualifications Framework
ASEAN	Association of Southeast Asian Nations
ATS	Apprenticeship Training Scheme
BIAC	Business and Industry Advisory Committee
CAC	Central Apprenticeship Council
CAIC	Caribbean Association of Industry and Commerce
CANTA	Caribbean Association of National Training Agencies
CAP	Career Advancement Programme
CAPE	Caribbean Advanced Proficiency Examination
CARICOM	Caribbean Community
CAST	College of Arts, Science & Technology
CBET	Competency Based Education and Training
CCCJ	Council of Community Colleges of Jamaica
Cedefop	European Centre for the Development of Vocational Training
cegeps	colleges, institutes, applied science and technology (Qubec)
CIO	Chief Information Officer
COHSOD	Council for Human and Social Development
CPD	Continuing Professional Development
CSEC	Caribbean Secondary Education Certificate
CSME	CARICOM Single Market and Economy
CTE	Career and Technical Education

CTVET	Career, Technical Vocational Education and Training
CVQ	Caribbean Vocational Qualification
CVTS	Continuing Vocational Training Survey
CXC	Caribbean Examinations Council
DGE&T	Directorate General of Employment & Training
DLLR	Department of Labour, Licensing and Regulation
GDP	Gross Domestic Product
GNVQ	General National Vocational Qualification
GSAT	Grade Six Achievement Test
ECOWAS	Economic Community of West African States
EDPD	Examination Administration and Production Division
EFA	Education For All
ETF	European Training Foundation
EQF	European Qualifications Framework
EQFLL	European Qualifications Framework for Lifelong Learning
EU	European Union
HEART	Human Employment and Resource Training
HEI	Higher Education Institution
HRD	Human Resource Development
IALS	International Adult Literacy Survey
ICT	Information and Communication Technology
ILO	International Labour Organization
IOE	Institute of Education
ISCED	International Standard Classification of Education
IT	Information Technology
ITC	Information Technology and Communications
ITE	Institute of Technological Education
ITO	Industry Training Organization
ITUC	International Trade Union Confederation
JTB	Jamaica Tourist Board
LO	The Norwegian Confederation of Trade Unions
MDG	Millennium Development Goal
MHRD	Ministry of Human Resource Development

MOE	Ministry of Education
NCQV	National Council for Vocational Qualifications
NCTVET	National Council on Technical and Vocational Education and Training
NCVER	National Centre for Vocational Education Research
NDET	Norwegian Directorate for Education and Training
NGO	Non-Governmental Organization
NHO	Confederation of Norwegian Enterprise
NSW	New South Wales
NTA	National Training Agency
NTB	National Training Board
NQF	National Qualifications Framework
NVQ-J	National Vocational Qualifications of Jamaica
OA	Office of Apprenticeship
OECD	Organization for Economic Co-operation and Development
OJT	On the Job training
PIOJ	Planning Institute of Jamaica
QF	Qualification Framework
RAP	Registered Apprenticeship Programme
RCMTVET	Regional Coordinating Mechanism for TVET
SAAs	State Apprenticeship Agencies
SADC	Southern African Development Community
SL-TOP	School Leavers Training Opportunities Programme
STATIN	Statistical Institute of Jamaica
STEM	Science, Technology, Engineering and Mathematics
TEC	Tertiary Education Commission
TEF	Tourism Enhancement Fund
TPDCo	Tourism Product Development Company
TQF	Transnational Qualification Framework
TQM	Total Quality Management
TVET	Technical Vocational Education and Training
UCJ	University Council of Jamaica
UIL	UNESCO's Institute for Lifelong Learning
UK	United Kingdom

UNDESD	United Nations Decade of Education for Sustainable Development
UNDP	United Nations Development Programme
UNESCO	United Nations Educational, Scientific and Cultural Organization
UNWTO	United Nations World Tourism Organization
USDOL	United States Department of Labour
USE	Universal Secondary Education
UTech	University of Technology, Jamaica
UWI	University of the West Indies
VET	Vocational Education Training
VT	Vocational Training
VTC	Vocational Training Centre
VTDI	Vocational Training Development Institute
VTF	Vocational Training Frameworks
VUSSC	Virtual University for Small States of the Commonwealth
WB	World Bank (WB)
WBL	Work-based learning
WFD	Workforce Development
WSDLI	Washington State Dept. of Labour & Industries
WTTC	World Travel and Tourism Council

CONTRIBUTORS

Professor Halden A. Morris Career, technical vocational education and training. University of the West Indies, Mona campus, Jamaica. - editor

Mr. Wilbert M. Nunes is currently employed to the University of Technology, Jamaica (UTech) as Lecturer in the Faculty of Education and Liberal Studies in the School of Technical and Vocational Education. He holds a Diploma in Telecommunication and a Bachelors of Education in Industrial Technology from UTech. He also holds a Master of Science in Digital Electronics and is reading for his PhD in Education with emphasis on Leadership in Technical and Vocational Education and Training and Workforce Development at the University of the West Indies. Mr. Nunes has over 10 years of experience in the telecommunication industry as a technician and as a junior executive at Cable and Wireless Jamaica now FLOW and over 10 years as a technical educator at the secondary and tertiary levels in Jamaica. He has been integral in the development of the Industrial Educators Association of Jamaica (ITEAJ) and is currently the president. He is also a member of the International Technology and Engineering Educators Association (ITEEA) and the Association of Technology, Management and Applied Engineering (ATMAE).

Dr. Carole M. Powell is currently Adjunct Lecturer for Leadership in TVET and Workforce Development (WFD), in the Faculty of Humanities and Education, School of Education UWI Mona, as well as Associate Consultant with the Facilitation and Consultancy Training Services (FACTS) Limited www.factshrd-cbss.com. She is former Director of the TVET Rationalization in Secondary Schools Pilot Project, a joint responsibility of The Jamaican Ministry of Education and the National Training Agency HEART Trust/NTA. Dr. Powell is also a former Principal of St. Andrew Technical High School and Table Leader for CXC Markers of Mathematics. Dr. Powell currently serves on the Quality Assurance Committee of the National Council on TVET (NCTVET) in Jamaica and is a Past President and founding member of Jamaica Association for TVET (JATVET). She is responsible for the conceptual preparation of "A Policy for TVET in Jamaican Secondary Schools". Additionally, she is a past President and Central Committee member of Jamaica Red Cross.

Mrs. Elaine I. Shakes is a Technical and Vocational Education and Training (TVET) professional with over thirty years of experience at the practitioner, administrative and managerial levels. She is a past Assistant Registrar/Syllabus and Curriculum development for the Caribbean Examinations Council where she held and managed successfully the portfolio for TVET and the Caribbean Vocational Qualifications (CVQ). Mrs. Shakes also served successfully as a manager in one of the HEART Trust/NTA institutions and was the recipient of the 2001 and 2002 Boss of the Year Award. She holds a Master of Science degree in Educational Leadership, a Bachelor of Education and Diploma in Technical Education and a Teacher's Certificate in Vocational Mathematics, Technical Drawing and English. Mrs. Shakes is currently reading for her MPHIL/PHD in Education with emphasis on Leadership in TVET and Workforce Development at the University of the West Indies.

Mr. Abdul A. Antoine is currently employed to the University of Technology, Jamaica (UTech) as a Lecturer in the School of Technical and Vocational Education within the Faculty of Education and Liberal Studies. Mr. Antoine specializes in

Mechanical Technology and is a former Director of Programmes for the B.Ed. in Industrial Technology. He has over 10 years experience as a technical educator at the secondary level and over 25 years experience at the tertiary level, in the Caribbean, and has supervised students' research projects at both the undergraduate and masters levels. Mr. Antoine holds a Bachelors of Education in Industrial Technology (Mechanical) from UTech; a Master of Science in Training and Development from the Illinois State University (USA); and he is presently pursuing TVET-related doctoral studies at the University of the West Indies (Mona).

Mr. Sheldon A. Thomas is currently a Vice Principal at Ferncourt High School, Claremont, St. Ann, Jamaica. He holds a Master of Science in Digital Technology from University of the West Indies, Mona and Bachelor of Education in Industrial Technology from University of Technology, Jamaica and is currently pursuing his MPHIL/PHD in Education with emphasis on Leadership in TVET and Workforce Development at the University of the West Indies. He has over 10 years of teaching experience at the secondary level. His research interests include Technical and Vocational Education and Training (TVET) and Science, Technology, Engineering and Mathematics.

INDEX

W

Printed in the United States
By Bookmasters